GREAT WALKS
YORKSHIRE DALES

GREAT WALKS

YORKSHIRE DALES

FRANK DUERDEN
Photography by David Ward

This special edition has been
produced in 1992
by New Orchard Editions Ltd,
Villiers House, 41/47 Strand,
London WC2N 5JE,
a Cassell company
for publication
by Printwise Publications Ltd,
47 Bradshaw Road, Tottington,
Bury, Lancs BL8 3PW

Reprinted 1993, 1994

Designed by Niki fforde

Maps based upon the Ordnance Survey map
with the Sanction of the Controller of Her
Majesty's Stationery Office.

Printed and bound by Graficromo S.A., Spain

ISBN 1-87222633-7

Contents

Acknowledgments   6
Introduction   7

THE YORKSHIRE DALES NATIONAL PARK   9

Facts and Figures   12
The face of the Yorkshire Dales   13
    Drystone walls   13
    Farming in the Dales   14
    Features of limestone country   16
    Lead mining   18
    The Dales underground   20
    Stiles, signposts and waymarks   20

SELECTED WALKS IN THE YORKSHIRE DALES NATIONAL PARK

Introduction to the route descriptions   24
Selected routes in order of increasing difficulty:

1. EASY ROUTES
    1. To Malham Cove   28
    2. Aysgarth Falls   33
    3. Cautley Spout   37
    4. Around Semer Water   42
    5. Clapham Beck to Ingleborough
        Cave   45
    6. The Waterfalls Walk   49
    7. To Hardraw Force   54
    8. Upper Wharfedale   59
    9. Gordale Scar and Malham
        Cove   64

2. MODERATE ROUTES
    10. Bolton Abbey and the Strid   70
    11. Hawkswick Moor   75
    12. The Ascent of Pen-y-ghent   79
    13. The Ascent of Ingleborough   84
    14. Upper Swaledale   90
    15. The Ascent of Whernside   97
    16. Crummack Dale and the Norber
        Erratics   103
    17. A Round of Malham Moor   108
    18. Carlton Moor   115
    19. Gunnerside and Hard Level
        Gills   120

3. MORE STRENUOUS ROUTES
    20. Simon's Seat and the Valley of
        Desolation   127
    21. Arkengarthdale   133
    22. The Calf and the Eastern
        Howgills   139
    23. Between Littondale and
        Wharfedale   145
    24. Mastiles Lane   151
    25. A Round of Barden Moor   157
    26. Wensleydale and Coverdale   163
    27. Tan Hill Inn and Melbecks
        Moor   169

4. VERY STRENUOUS ROUTE
    28. The Three Peaks Walk   178

APPENDICES

Access for the walker   186
Safety   187
Giving a grid reference   188
Countryside Access Charter   189
Addresses of useful organizations   190

Index   192

ACKNOWLEDGMENTS

The preparation of this book, including the original edition, has taken up most of my spare time over a total period of about two years. It has been made considerably easier and certainly far more enjoyable by the kindness and help that I have received from many people, most of whom live in the Dales area.

In particular, I thank the staff of the Yorkshire Dales National Park Authority who gave a great deal of their time to ensure that my manuscript was accurate and as up-to-date as possible. Mr. T. Harper formerly of Ghyll Farm, Sedbergh read through the section on farming and Dr. Yvonne Williams of The Polytechnic of North London, helped me with the sections on the geology.

I have to thank the Countryside Commission for permission to include the Countryside Access Charter. Some information has been included from the initial National Park Plan. The maps were drawn from 1:25 000 maps with the permission of the Ordnance Survey.

Finally, I must thank Mrs. Jennifer Peck and my daughters, Beverley and Sharon, for typing the manuscripts, and my wife, Audrey, who helped me with proof-reading.

INTRODUCTION

I consider myself very fortunate to have spent my early years in Nelson, a textile town on the extreme northern edge of the Lancashire industrial belt. For not only did it possess an extremely fine cricket team — arguably perhaps the most famous league team in the world due to its long and very successful association with Learie Constantine — but it also lay within easy reach of the moors of the central and northern Pennines. My twin loves of cricket and of walking undoubtedly grew out of those early associations.

I cannot in all honesty claim that my career as a cricketer disturbed the sleep of many established players. I saw myself then — and certainly do nowadays — essentially in the role of a spectator. My love of walking however has, I am glad to say, taken an altogether more active form and I look back now over thirty-five years full of extremely happy days spent out in the countryside, a high proportion of which were in wild and lonely places.

As Nelson is a mere 11 miles from the southern boundary of what is now the Yorkshire Dales National Park — the Park was not designated until 1954 — visits there, even in those car-less days, were made at frequent intervals. Malham, Gordale, Hawes, Settle and Ingleton have been well-known and well-loved places for as long as I can remember, and the three peaks of Ingleborough, Pen-y-ghent and Whernside found a place on my list of favourite mountains from the beginning. To me the Yorkshire Dales have always held a special place.

It is doubtful if any other region of the British Isles has experienced such an increase in popularity in recent years as the Yorkshire Dales. This is due largely — if not entirely — to the books of James Herriot, to the very successful television series *All Creatures Great and Small* which was based upon them and, more recently, to the publication of *James Herriot's Yorkshire*. I shared accommodation recently in a Wensleydale cottage with a family from the American mid-west. They were sparing a few days there from a crowded schedule specifically because they had read and so much enjoyed James Herriot's stories.

Yorkshire folk — who have a well-deserved reputation for hard-headedness and for knowing a good thing when they see it — have, of course, always visited the Dales in droves; nearly one in three of those taking their holidays there are from Yorkshire. To Yorkshiremen and Yorkshirewomen home is still best, apparently, whether at work or play.

Above all, however, few have more appreciated the Dales through the years than walkers and ramblers, for the beauty of the area has always been best revealed to those who left the roads and followed the footpaths up to the loneliness of the high fells.

There are approximately 1100 miles (1770 km) of public footpaths and bridleways within the area of the Park — this book describes about 20% of them. Those who know the area well will appreciate that it was not an easy task to select twenty-eight routes which give excellent walking, which are representative of the diverse countryside of the Dales, which offer a range of difficulty and length for walkers of differing ability, which give — on clear days — some of the finest views, which visit some of the most interesting places within the Park, and finally which are free of any access problems. I would be pleased to hear, through my publisher, from anyone who can suggest changes to the list or modifications to the routes, which might be incorporated into future editions.

In some cases an excellent walk was omitted because, at the moment, there is some doubt about access. Whether we like it or not, walkers do not have the right to walk anywhere they wish within the National Park and some farmers quite correctly object to walkers crossing their land, away from public footpaths, without permission. One hears, unfortunately, stories of damaged walls and rudeness from walkers — usually involving a party — when confronted by farmers. The price for damage or rudeness is often paid by later walkers or by the National Park Wardens who receive the complaints. This is not to imply, of course, that all farmers are angels, but merely to point out that walkers also have a responsibility towards the countryside, which some of them, unfortunately, abuse.

I have been very fortunate during the preparation of this edition, in working with a photographer, David Ward, who obviously sees the Dales in the same way that I do. If, eventually, in extreme old age, my memory does begin to slip away, his superb photographs will, I am sure, bring the beauty of the Yorkshire Dales back to me with all its present clarity.

FRANK DUERDEN

THE YORKSHIRE DALES NATIONAL PARK

John Dower defined a National Park as 'an extensive area of beautiful and relatively wild country in which, for the nation's benefit and by appropriate national decision and action, (a) the characteristic landscape beauty is strictly preserved, (b) access and facilities for public open-air enjoyment are amply provided, (c) wild life and buildings and places of architectural and historic interest are suitably protected, while (d) established farming use is effectively maintained.'

Under the National Parks and Access to the Countryside Act of 1949 a National Parks Commission was established which was responsible for the creation of National Parks; ten were created by the Commission in England and Wales between 1950 and 1957. In 1968 the National Parks Commission was replaced by the Countryside Commission which thereupon took over responsibility for the Parks. A further change came under the Local Government Act of 1972; under this Act a separate National Park Authority was set up for each National Park charged with its administration. Each Authority was given the task of producing a National Park Plan by 1st April, 1977, and of reviewing the plan at intervals of not more than five years. This set out the policies of the Authority for the management of its Park and proposals for carrying out those policies.

The National Park Authorities are charged with two main aims: to preserve and enhance the natural beauty of the areas designated as National Parks; and to encourage the provision or improvement of facilities for the enjoyment of open-air recreation and the study of nature within the National Parks. The Authorities must in addition have due regard for the social and economic needs of the people living and working within them.

It cannot be too strongly emphasized that the area covered by a Park is not 'acquired' by the nation. In the Yorkshire Dales National Park, for example, less than one per cent of the area is under any form of public ownership, the rest is owned and used by private farmers and landowners.

The Yorkshire Dales National Park Committee acts as local planning authority for the area and in that it is no different from other local planning authorities throughout England and Wales. Generally, it seeks to work by agreement and co-operation with local owners and occupiers, using compulsory powers only

FIGURE 1 *The Yorkshire Dales National Park. The map shows the boundary, main towns and villages, and the more important roads within and around the area of the park.*

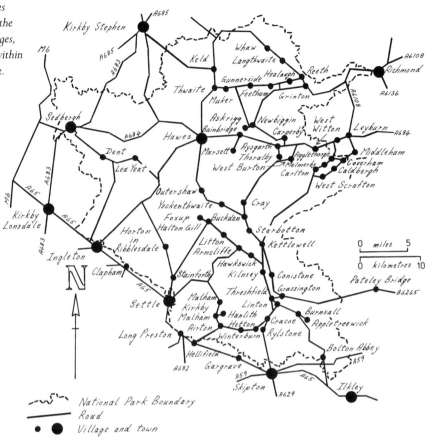

when these fail. Even these compulsory powers are limited in their scope. In the end therefore the Committee relies to a high degree on the goodwill of others.

The overall management of the Park is the responsibility of the Yorkshire Dales National Park Committee. This has twenty-four members, of which twelve are County Councillors of the North Yorkshire County Council, one is a County Councillor of Cumbria County Council, three are District Councillors from the Craven, Richmondshire and South Lakeland District Councils and eight are appointed by the Secretary of State for the Environment (after consultation with the Countryside Commission).

The Committee acts through a team of full-time and part-time staff headed by the National Park Officer. Two Assistant National Park Officers are responsible for the working of offices at Bainbridge in Wensleydale and Grassington in Wharfedale. A Head Warden and six Area Wardens are supported in their work by a number of voluntary wardens.

National Park Centres, which will provide information to

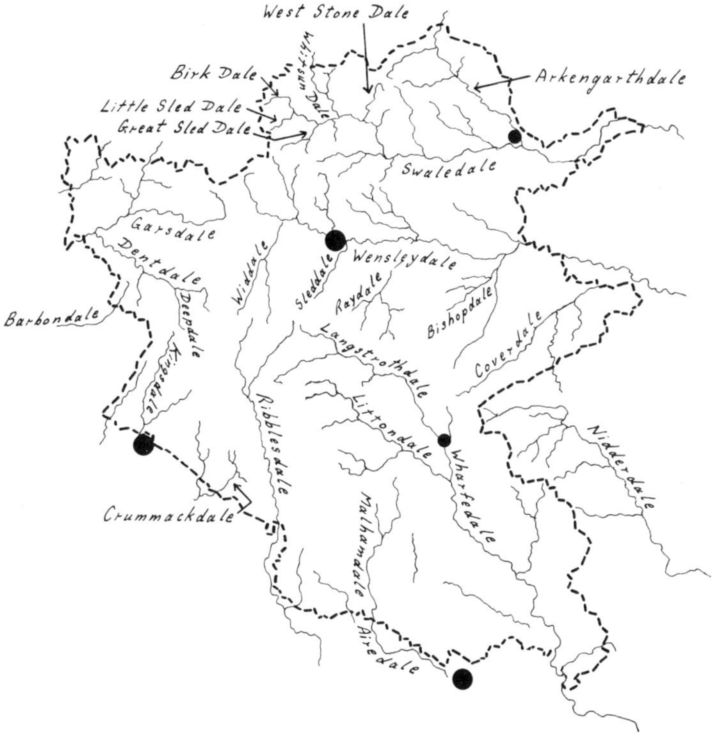

FIGURE 2 *The principal dales of the National Park area.*

visitors, are at:

Aysgarth Falls   Wensleydale (0969) 663 424
Clapham   Clapham (046 85) 419
Grassington   Grassington (0756) 752748
Hawes   Wensleydale (0969) 667 450
Malham   Airton (072 93) 363
Sedbergh   Sedbergh (053 96) 20125

These are open April-October inclusive. Opening times do vary to some extent from year to year and from centre to centre, but generally they are open daily during this period. There are also a number of information points through the park.

Those interested in acting as guides on programmed walks or as voluntary wardens should contact the National Park Office at Grassington.

SOME FACTS AND FIGURES ABOUT THE YORKSHIRE DALES NATIONAL PARK

DESIGNATED   1954. The Park was the seventh of the ten Parks to be designated.

AREA   680 square miles (176 119 hectares). It is the third largest; only the Lake District and Snowdonia National Parks are larger.

	Approximately one eighth of this is in Cumbria, the rest is in North Yorkshire.
EMBLEM	The head of a Swaledale tup (ram). The design was based upon a photograph of the best tup at Muker Show in 1974.
POPULATION	There are approximately 18,000 people living within the area of the Park.

WHERE VISITORS COME FROM (%)

England	Day trips	Holidays
Yorkshire/Humberside	65	32
North-West	16	17
Northern	16	12
East Midlands	1	6
South-East	0.5	16
East Anglia	0.3	4
West Midlands	0.2	5
South-West	0.1	2
Scotland	0.6	3
Wales	0.4	2
Overseas	0	1

About eight million people visit the National Park each year; some 90 per cent of these stay for less than six hours.

THE FACE OF THE YORKSHIRE DALES

DRYSTONE WALLS

There is probably no feature of the Yorkshire Dales that attracts the attention of visitors more than do the drystone walls. They form crazy patterns around the villages, run along and across valleys, climb boldly up the fell sides and mark the line of ridges and of summits. They are called drystone walls because they were built entirely without mortar, their strength and durability products only of the skill and craft of the men who built them.

Although there are records of some walling in the thirteenth century, the building of stone walls was not extensive until the sixteenth when it became the custom for villagers to build them around their holdings. The crazy pattern of small irregular fields now found around villages such as Malham is characteristic of this period. Most of the walls however were built in the late eighteenth and early nineteenth centuries when vast areas of land were being enclosed by Act of Parliament. The long straight walls of the open fell were the products of this legislation. This movement was not confined to the Dales, nor indeed was this area the most affected, but nevertheless the change must have been considerable. With some exceptions the wall pattern of the Dales was established by about 1820.

Stone was plentiful and near-to-hand in most areas of the Dales, but as approximately one ton was needed for each square yard of wall, the work was hard and called for judgment to avoid unnecessary labour. A waller would usually work with an assistant, one to each side of the wall, with their material stacked nearby. It was a job for the warmer months of the year for cold winds, driving rain and snow made the work too difficult at other times.

The line of the wall would be marked out with pegs and string and if necessary a trench cut to receive a level and firm foundation of large and heavy stones. Upon this the wall would be built, five or six feet high, the shape, size and direction being maintained by two frames with straining cords between. The wall would be built sloping inwards towards the top for extra stability, and two stones wide with occasional through or tie stones inserted through the full width to bind them together. Smaller stones would be used to fill the gap in the centre and any in the sides. Finally, large flat stones were used at the top to level the wall before a coping or capping was added made up of flat, rounded stones placed on edge.

FARMING IN THE DALES

The Yorkshire Dales is predominantly an area of permanent grass and rough grazing, only a very small proportion being regularly ploughed. The farming is therefore almost entirely pastoral, devoted to the rearing of sheep and cattle.

About one third of the farms, particularly those in the valleys where the grazing is richer, concentrate on dairy farming, whilst the higher hill farms, having to contend with the harsher conditions of the fells, are concerned almost entirely with sheep. Intermediate farms will keep both sheep and beef herds. It has been estimated that in a typical summer there are over half a million ewes and lambs within the Park and about 75,000 cattle and calves. These produce sufficient milk, beef and lamb for about a half million people, an output worth more than eleven million pounds annually.

The Swaledale and the Dalesbred are the breeds of sheep most commonly encountered in the Dales, although several other types are also stocked. The Swaledale, first raised in the harsh conditions of the Northern Dales but now bred over a much wider area, is one of Britain's toughest breed of sheep, with the possible exceptions of the Herdwick and the Rough Fell. It is of medium size, with an outer fleece of long, coarse, stringy locks, the face black or dark grey (sometimes with light patches) and white nose, the legs mottled black. Both rams and ewes have strong horns curving roughly in a helical form. The Dalesbred originated as a cross between Swaledale and Scottish Blackface, but is now regarded as a breed in its own right. It is very similar to the former but distinguished by the white patches on each side of the nose.

It is common practice to cross ewes of mountain and moorland breeds with rams of more fertile breeds to produce ewes with a higher birthrate and a better milk yield. These may then be further crossed with a downland ram such as a Suffolk or Dorset to increase body size. In this way the good qualities of each breed are combined together in the progeny. A cross between a Swaledale or Dalesbred ewe with a Blue Faced Leicester ram is known as a Mule or Greyface and that with a Teeswater or Wensleydale is a Masham.

Lambing mainly takes place in April but will continue until mid-May on the higher farms; two lambs for each ewe is common in the valleys with the fertility dropping off with increasing altitude. Lambing usually takes place in fields near to the farm where the pasture is better, but as soon as possible afterwards the ewe and her lambs are driven up to the fell, for the meadows are required to produce a valuable crop of hay.

During the latter half of June and into July the flock is gathered again, when older sheep are sheared (almost entirely by machine), each ewe producing about 4 lb (1.8 kg) of wool.

At the end of summer in September the sheep are again collected. Ewes who have had three lambing seasons and whose teeth are failing, are sold to lowland farms where they may produce lambs for one or two years more. Lambs, not required to maintain the breeding flock, are sold for immediate slaughter or to lowland farms for fattening or breeding.

During the winter the breeding flock of ewes stays on the fell, to be gathered and brought down only when heavy snow is likely or when lambing becomes imminent. In October and November they run with the rams, normally about one ram for every 50 to 60 ewes, and the breeding cycle begins again.

Dairy herds are fed on the best pastures of a farm during the summer months, but in the winter they are confined to shippons to escape the rigours of the weather where they are fed on hay and silage with barley or oats. There is also a good trade in beef cattle, raised on hill farms and sold later to lowland farms for fattening before slaughter. The most common breeds are the Friesian (large heavy animals coloured black and white in distinct patches with short horns curling forwards and inwards) and the Northern Dairy Shorthorn (usually light roan with short curved horns tilted upwards). The first is primarily a dairy breed, with a higher milk yield than any other, whilst the second is regarded as dual-purpose. It should be noted that nowadays most calves are dehorned. Milking in the Dales, as elsewhere, is becoming increasingly mechanized, the average yield for a cow being about 3 gallons (13.6 litres) per day over a nine month period each year.

FEATURES OF LIMESTONE COUNTRY

The rocks which most determine the general features of the Yorkshire Dales are sedimentary, laid down during the Carboniferous period between 350 and 220 million years ago. For much of this period the Dales were covered by sea, although it would be a time of repeated advance and retreat of the sea with major areas clear for substantial periods rather than one of complete and continuous submergence. The deposits laid down on the sea-bed over those long periods of time produced these sedimentary rocks.

The first (and now the lowest) bed formed in the Carboniferous Period was of limestone, which was given the name Great Scar Limestone because of its responsibility for the enormous scars or cliffs to the south of the Park. It was formed out of the skeletal remains of life forms which abounded in the clear and shallow seas of the early Carboniferous and now covers the Park in a thick and substantially horizontal layer. The rocks which lie over this, the Yoredale Series made up from thin layers of mudstones, sandstones, siltstones and limestones, were laid down in the conditions of a river-delta, with its constantly changing pattern of mudflats, sand banks and sea. The final and highest bed is of Millstone Grit; a dark, coarse, resistant rock, laid down towards the end of the Carboniferous Period.

The Great Scar Limestone dominates the scenery to the south-west of the Park around Malham, Settle and Ingleton where most of the overlying rocks have been stripped away and the thickness of the limestone exposed by faulting; the peaks of Ingleborough and Pen-y-ghent owing their shape and existence to their small caps of Millstone Grit. To the north the plane of the limestone dips away so that the predominant rocks of Wensleydale and Swaledale are those of the Yoredale Series.

The limestone region of the south-west is a typical example of karst country; similar terrain to this can be found in Yugoslavia and Italy on the shore of the Adriatic — from where the name 'Karst' originates — in south-west France and Andalusia in Spain. The common feature of all these regions being the presence of limestone on or near to the surface.

Limestone is a hard rock, composed largely of calcium carbonate, and characterized by extensive vertical cracking (joints). It is virtually insoluble in pure water. Rain and stream water can however absorb carbon dioxide from the air to form a weak acid solution which will dissolve limestone, the product being calcium bicarbonate. Because of this effect, flowing water with dissolved carbon dioxide is called aggressive water. Evaporation, however, of bicarbonate-saturated water will cause some of the bicarbonate to change back again into carbonate, which being insoluble in water is then re-deposited. It is these two processes of solution and re-deposition over a long period of time which produce the characteristic features of karst country.

SINKHOLES

A sinkhole is a funnel-shaped depression in the ground usually from 10 to 30 feet (3 to 9 m) in depth. It may be formed by the sudden collapse of rock over an underground cavern, but more often by the slow solution of the underlying limestone as aggressive water percolates down through the joints, causing the soil layer to gradually subside.

DRY CREEKS AND WATER-SINKS

Horizontal limestone beds, such as the Great Scar Limestone, are so effective at removing water which eventually finds its way down the joints, that it is rare for a surface stream to flow for any distance over it. The point where a stream disappears underground is called its sink. In some cases this is a substantial open shaft (called a swallow or pot-hole), but in other cases the stream sinks slowly into the ground without any opening being obvious. In either case a dry creek — and sometimes dry waterfalls — are left below the sink which mark the old line of the stream. The stream continues its course underground, eventually emerging some distance away; the point where the stream re-appears is called its rise (or resurgence). In times of exceptionally heavy rain, when the underground passages can no longer cope with the flow, the stream may resume its former path, to disappear again when the flow falls.

CAVES AND POT-HOLES

Water action along the horizontal bedding planes and the vertical joints of the limestone has become so advanced in some cases that extensive cave systems have developed. Gaping Gill, on the south-west slopes of Ingleborough, has a main chamber 110 feet (33 m) high and passages which have been explored over a distance of $6\frac{1}{2}$ miles (10.5 km).

The beauty of cave systems is much enhanced by the formation of stalactites, which hang like icicles from the roof, and stalagmites which are formed beneath on the cave floor. These are caused by re-deposition of calcium carbonate. Water seeping drop by drop through small crevices in the roof, partially evaporates leaving behind a small deposit of calcium carbonate, which gradually builds up to form a stalactite. Stalagmites are formed in a similar manner by water dropping onto the floor of the cave. Stalagmites are always broader than stalactites due to the splashing that takes place when the drops fall. Eventually the two may unite to form a vertical pillar.

PAVEMENTS
The effect of weathering can be seen most clearly where the upper surface of the Great Scar Limestone has been exposed, such as at Malham Cove and on Ingleborough. These areas are usually referred to as limestone pavements, because of their appearance. The joints in the limestone have been widened by water solution to form a pattern of isolated blocks surrounded by crevices usually 9 to 12 inches (20–30 cm) wide and up to 12 feet (3.7 m) in depth. Occasionally the water has also penetrated horizontally along a lower bedding plane so that a block becomes totally detached and will wobble when stepped upon. The vertical crevices are called grikes and the isolated blocks clints. The upper surface of a clint is sometimes flat, but more usually worn into smooth grooves, called runnels, caused by water running from the top surface of the clint into the grike. The grikes themselves offer an ideal habitat for plants — damp, sheltered and protected — and are a treasure-house for the botanist.

Lead Mining

The mining and the extraction of lead were carried out largely in two areas of the Yorkshire Dales; the first to the north and south of Swaledale between Keld and Marrick, and the second to the east of Wharfedale, in particular over Greenhow Hill towards Nidderdale, between Appletreewick and Cray.

Lead mining in the Dales goes back at least to the second century AD, for pigs of lead bearing dates and the names of Roman Emperors have been found there, but it is very likely that some mining took place at an earlier date. It also continued, if only intermittently, from that time for there are many later records of the metal being used in roofing and extant accounts of output and the conveyancing of mining rights. The real rise of the industry began however very much later during the sixteenth century. Changes of ownership, the injection of capital and the development of mining techniques combined with increase in demand to produce an expansion which reached its peak towards the end of the eighteenth and the beginning of the nineteenth centuries. Late in the nineteenth century the industry declined sharply; exhaustion of existing seams, escalating costs of extraction and the importation of cheaper supplies

from abroad being the main causes. Most mines had ceased production by about 1885, although a few were able to continue working into this century.

The lead ore, mainly galena or lead sulphide, occurred in veins at an average concentration of about 5 per cent, the main vein material, which had no commercial value, being referred to as gangue. As with other metallic ores the galena did not occur uniformly, but could peter out and then increase again in concentration further along a vein; a fact which accounts for the varying fortunes of the mines. The methods employed in extraction were in no way unique to the Dales. Once a vein had been located a shaft was sunk and horizontal passages, called levels, driven off at suitable depths. Levels could also be driven off horizontally into steep hillsides without the preliminary digging of a shaft if a suitable valley crossed the mining area.

A common feature of the mining areas are hushes, which are gullies produced in the search for fresh veins. A likely stream would be dammed at a high point, then the water released as a torrent to strip away the top soil so that a close examination of the ground could be made.

The extracted ore was first dressed, i.e. sorted to remove as much gangue as possible, broken into small pieces, and then smelted, i.e. heated with wood or coal to oxidize and then reduce the ore to the metal.

The levels and the old buildings of the mines are still obvious around Swaledale and Wharfedale, although the passage of time has had, of course, its usual way upon them. The buildings can be explored in safety; the open mouths of hillside levels, however tempting, cannot, except by those who have both the experience and the equipment to deal with their dangers. But do not let this limitation put you off, the extant workings of Blakethwaite Mill, Surrender and Old Gang are still well worth the visit.

THE DALES UNDERGROUND

Serious caving is usually considered to have begun with the descent of Gaping Gill by Edward Martel in 1895 (see page 88), although there are records of earlier attempts to explore well-known cave openings. The pursuit was popular in the Pennines throughout the first half of this century, but as with so many other outdoor pursuits the years since World War II have seen an enormous increase in the number of active participants. Today there are probably about 16,000 active cavers in Britain, belonging to some 400 clubs.

Of the four major caving areas in Britain — Yorkshire, Derbyshire, the Mendips in Somerset and South Wales — the first is undoubtedly the most important, both in the number and in the severity of its cave systems. It has been estimated that there are over 600 known caves in the Northern Pennine Cave Area, which is centred on the National Park, containing some 200 miles (322 km) of passages. Although the word 'cave' is used in a general sense to describe all such systems, cavers generally distinguish between 'caves' which contain horizontal passages and 'pot-holes' which have vertical pitches requiring the use of special equipment.

Standard equipment for the caver is protective helmet, cap lamp (carbide or electric with rechargeable battery), boiler suit or neoprene foam wet suit, knee-pads and rubber-soled boots. Horizontal or near-horizontal passages of low height can be negotiated by crawling or squeezing along, vertical shafts by the use of light-weight caving ladders or the employment of special techniques borrowed from the climbing world of abseiling-down and prusiking-up single or doubled ropes. Pools and flowing streams have to be waded through; if the roof dips for a short distance below the water surface then a 'duck' becomes necessary or, if the distance is longer, a dive. The use of cave diving techniques with air cylinders for long flooded passages is a more advanced — and also a far more hazardous — specialization.

STILES, SIGNPOSTS AND WAYMARKS

The word 'stile' comes from the Old English word 'stigel' which means 'to climb'. In an area such as the Yorkshire Dales with its profusion of walls they are a very important feature.

The traditional 'drystone wall' stiles of the Dales fall into two basic patterns. In the first, a small gap is left at the top of the wall (up to one third of the total height) and two, three or four through-stones, projecting on both sides are set to form steps up to it. In the second, a gap is left through the full height of the wall just wide enough to allow a person to squeeze through. Frequently this is closed with a small gate. A common variation is to make the stile somewhat wider (about 2 feet/60 cm) and reduce its width in the lower half to perhaps 6 inches (15 cm) or so by two narrow rectangular slabs placed vertically one to each side. The square openings, left in the base of a wall and closed with a slab, are called 'cripple holes' and were left to allow sheep to be transferred from one side to the other.

In recent years a considerable number of wooden ladder stiles have been placed over walls on public footpaths and at a few strategic places by the National Park Authority. These can usually be picked out at a distance and are a valuable aid in route-finding where the paths are faint. In a few areas, particularly around villages, kissing gates have been erected as an alternative to ladder stiles.

Highway Authorities have a duty to erect signs at any point where a footpath or bridleway leaves a metalled road, and the power to place waymarks at the ends or along the length of a way. The National Park Authority has an active programme of signposting and waymarking, although the resources that can be allocated to this are very limited. In general, priority is given to long distance routes crossing the area of the Park and to inter-dale routes. A large number of carved wooden signposts have been erected; these are made from Iroka, an imported wood with particularly good weathering resistance. Waymarking follows the Countryside Commission recommendation: a foot-path (for walkers only) is marked with yellow marks and arrows and a bridleway (for walkers, cyclists and horse riders) with blue marks and arrows. A few paths on high ground with particular problems of route-finding have been marked with posts and placed at regular intervals. Moorland paths are also commonly marked by cairns (built by local farmers and ramblers, not by the Authority).

SELECTED WALKS IN THE YORKSHIRE DALES NATIONAL PARK

Introduction to the Route Descriptions

---

1. Access (see page 186)

The majority of walks are along paths for which there is public right-of-way, or which cross moors covered by a current access agreement. Six cross private ground where access is allowed on payment of a small fee (these are indicated). In addition to these, one or two routes have been included to which the above does not apply, but which have, as far as is known, been walked for a long time without objection and it is not expected therefore that difficulties will be encountered. Nevertheless, responsibility must rest with the walker in such cases to obtain any appropriate permission before commencing a walk. 'Short cuts' that might lead to proliferation of paths or to the annoyance of local people should not be taken. Paths are sometimes diverted officially by the National Park Authority, for example to allow a badly-eroded path to recover. The diversion will usually be well-marked. In such cases, of course, the diversion should always be followed.

2. Ascent

The amount of climbing involved in each route has been estimated from Outdoor Leisure or 1:50 000 maps as appropriate and should be regarded as approximate only.

3. Car-Parks

The nearest public car-park is given. There will be many places where a car can be parked by the wayside, but it must be done with care, as indiscriminate parking can be a great nuisance to local people.

4. Interesting Features on the Route

The best position for seeing these is indicated both in the route descriptions and on the maps by *(1), (2)*, etc.

5. Length

These are strictly 'map miles' estimated from the Outdoor Leisure or 1:50 000 maps; no attempt has been made to take into account any ascent or descent involved.

6. Maps

The maps are drawn to a scale of approximately 1:25 000 (see page 25) and all names are as given on the Outdoor Leisure maps. Field boundaries in particular, which can be a mixture of hedge, fence and wall, should be taken as a 'best description'. The maps have been drawn in the main, so that the route goes from the bottom to the top of a page. This will enable the reader to 'line up' the map in the direction walked whilst still holding

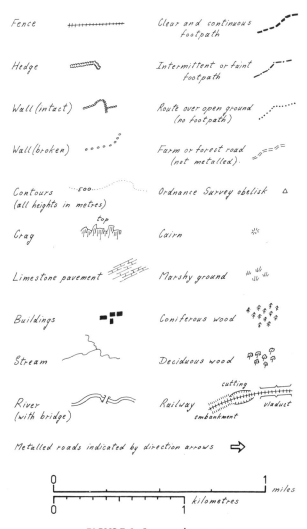

FIGURE 3 *Signs used on maps*

the book in the normal reading position. The arrow on each map points to grid north. The scale of some small features has been slightly exaggerated for clarity. For easy cross-reference, the relevant Outdoor Leisure and Landranger sheets are indicated on each map.

7. ROUTE DESCRIPTION

The letters 'L' and 'R' stand for left and right respectively. Where these are used for changes of direction then they imply a turn of about 90° when facing in the direction of the walk. 'Half L' and 'half R' indicate a half-turn, i.e. approximately 45°, and 'back half L' or 'back half R' indicate three quarter-turns, i.e. about 135°. PFS stands for 'Public Footpath Sign', PBS for 'Public Bridleway Sign' and OS for 'Ordnance Survey'.

To avoid constant repetition, it should be assumed that all

stiles and gates mentioned in the route description are to be crossed (unless there is a specific statement otherwise).

8. STANDARD OF THE ROUTES

The briefest examination of the route descriptions that follow will show that the routes described cover an enormous range of both length and of difficulty; the easiest can probably be undertaken by a family party at almost any time of the year whilst the hardest are only really suitable for experienced fell-walkers who are both fit and well-equipped. Any walker therefore who is contemplating following a route should make sure before starting that it is within his or her ability.

It is not easy in practice however to give an accurate picture of the difficulty of any route, because it is dependent upon a number of factors and will in any case vary considerably from day to day with the weather. Any consideration of weather conditions must, of course, be left to the walker himself (but read the section on safety first). Apart from that, it is probably best to attempt an overall assessment of difficulty based upon the length, amount of ascent and descent, problems of route-finding and finally, upon the roughness of the terrain.

Each of the routes has therefore been given a grading based upon a consideration of these factors and represented by the bold numerals which precedes each walk title. A general description of each grade follows:

Easy (1) Generally short walks (up to 5 miles, 8 km) over well-defined paths, with no problems of route-finding. Some climbing may be involved, but mostly over fairly gradual slopes with only short sections of more difficult ground.

Moderate (2) Rather longer walks (up to about 10 miles, 16 km), mostly over paths, but with sections where route-finding will be more difficult. Mountain summits may be reached with climbing over steeper and rougher ground.

More strenuous (3) Perhaps longer walks (10–20 miles, 16–32 km) with prolonged spells of climbing. Some rough ground, calling for good route-finding ability, perhaps with stretches of scrambling.

Very strenuous (4) Only for the few, involving long distances (over 20 miles, 32 km), with a considerable amount of climbing.

The walks are arranged in order of increasing difficulty, so that Route 1 is the easiest and Route 28 the hardest.

A summary of each walk is given at the head of each section with information on length, amount of climbing and any special difficulties, such as scrambling, that will be met along the way.

9. STARTING AND FINISHING POINTS

With one exception all the routes are circular, returning to their starting point, as this avoids any problems with transport when

FIGURE 4 *Starting points. The numbers indicate the starting points for the selected walks described later.*

the walk is completed. The location of each starting point is given by the number of the appropriate Landranger (1:50 000) map with a six figure grid reference (see page 188); thus (98-900627) indicates grid reference 900627 which can be found on Landranger sheet no. 98.

10. TIME FOR COMPLETION

The usual method of estimating the length of time needed for a walk is by Naismith's Rule; 'For ordinary walking allow one hour for every 3 miles (5 km) and add one hour for every 2000 feet (600 m) of ascent; for backpacking with a heavy load allow one hour for every 2½ miles (4 km) and one hour for every 1500 feet (450 m) of ascent'. However, for many this tends to be over-optimistic and it is better for each walker to form an assessment of his own performance over one or two walks. Naismith's Rule also makes no allowance for rest or food stops or for the influence of weather conditions.

TO MALHAM COVE

STARTING AND FINISHING POINT
Malham National Park Centre car-park (98-900627)
LENGTH
2 miles (3 km)
ASCENT
200 feet (60 m)

The Cove, a magnificent and overhanging precipice 240 feet (73 m) high is one of the most impressive sights in the Yorkshire Dales. It provided the inspiration for Charles Kingsley's *The Water Babies* and in more recent years has been the scene of some of the most difficult and exposed climbs on British limestone. The route from Malham to the Cove along the west side of Malham Beck is very popular, the return over pastures to the east is quieter and better.

ROUTE DESCRIPTION (Map 1)

Leave the large car-park in Malham *(1)* turning L down the minor road past the Information Centre. At the road turn L again and walk to the stone bridge at the centre of the village. Do not cross the bridge, but continue on the road ahead (signpost to Malham Tarn, Langcliffe and Settle). A few yards along, after the telephone box, turn R and then immediately L through a small gate (PFS 'Pennine Way'); this leads to a short

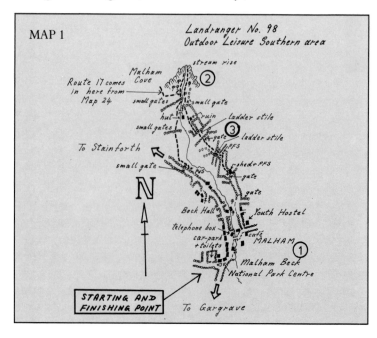

MAP 1

Landranger No. 98
Outdoor Leisure Southern area

but delightful path by the river which is a much better alternative to the road itself. Further along rejoin the road and continue in the same direction. After about 500 yards (460 m) from the bridge in Malham, pass a farmhouse on your R; here the road begins to climb steeply (road sign '1:7 single track road with passing places'). Follow the road up the hill; 175 yards (160 m) after a barn on the R go through a small gate in the wall to the R (Pennine Way sign).

The great cliff of Malham Cove can now be seen directly ahead. Follow the very clear path which heads directly for the Cove. The path crosses a wall at a small gate and then heads slightly R to the bank of the stream. Pass a footbridge, cross a second wall and continue along the bank to reach the cliff at its centre where the stream emerges (2). There are very few places within the Yorkshire Dales — or indeed anywhere, for that matter — more impressive than this spot at the foot of the Cove.

You can return from here by the same route, but it is much better instead to use a footpath on the opposite side of the stream. Cross the stream and walk down on the other bank to a small gate (PFS 'Malham $\frac{3}{4}$'). (When there is too much water to make the crossing, use the footbridge lower down.) At the small

Near Malham Cove. The walk returns to Malham along the opposite side of the stream.

29

gate do not go to the footbridge, but instead go on a path slightly L, soon climbing up a bank (yellow waymarks). At the top continue in the same direction with the steep slope of the bank to your R. Pass to the R of a ruined barn and then follow a wall to a ladder stile in a corner *(3)*. Cross the next field to a gate. Continue in the same direction to a PFS 'Malham/The Cove') and then to the L of a ruined (but substantial) wall, to a further ladder stile. Go between walls (PFS) and then half R across a narrow field to a gate by a small shed in the far L-hand corner (PFS 'Malham/The Cove'). Enter a walled lane and follow it back to Malham, reaching the village by the Youth Hostel.

1 Malham

The exact derivation of the name Malham is not clear, but it may mean 'stony or gravelly place', a name which would be in keeping with much of its surrounding area. In the Domesday Book the name is given as 'Malgun' whilst thirteenth century records show it as 'Malghum' or 'Malgum'. In any event there has been a settlement at Malham for well over one thousand years and human habitation in the area for perhaps three thousand. Today it is without doubt the most popular village in the National Park with one million visitors each year; partly because it is within easy reach of the large industrial towns to the south and east and partly because it is near to three of the most impressive features of the Dales, the Cove, the Tarn and Gordale Scar.

The present bridge which marks the centre of the village is eighteenth century but incorporates much of an earlier pack-horse bridge of the seventeenth, while there are three clapper bridges of earlier origin. The Buck Inn is comparatively recent, but Lister's Arms bears the date 1723. Beck Hall by the road to the Cove is Tudor. The Youth Hostel is one of a chain of hostels along the Pennine Way and the largest in the Park.

2 Malham Cove

The Middle Craven Fault, running roughly east to west just north of Malham, marks the southern limit of the Great Scar Limestone, for the land to the south of it is of a very different character. The Cove and the valley in front of it were created when glacial melt waters ran down the steep hillside produced by the fault and eroded back cutting into the edge of the limestone bed. It is a magnificent sight: a great natural amphitheatre with sheer — and, in parts, overhanging —

Malham Cove

walls tapering back into the hillsides on each side. The stream of icy water issuing from its foot sank underground at Smelt Mill Sink about $1\frac{1}{2}$ miles (2.5 km) to the north-west. As at Gordale Scar house martins build their nests each year under the great overhangs and the birds are a familiar sight in June wheeling and swooping over the huge face.

Magnificent as it may still be, the Cove has, in fact, lost a little of its glory over the years, for the depression in the centre of the cliff was originally the lip of a waterfall, about three times higher than any existing fall in the Dales today. Not since the early years of the nineteenth century however has any water been known to flow over it.

To the rock climber the Cove is the finest crag in the Dales, with about one hundred routes up to 600 feet (180 m) in length. The huge and very impressive Central Wall, directly above the stream exit, was first climbed in 1959.

3 *Iron-Age field boundaries*
The first two fields after leaving the road on the walk to Malham Cove are crossed by a series of parallel ridges running down the hillside towards the stream. These are the remains of Iron-Age field boundaries probably worked about the third century AD. Similar remains can be found at other sites in the Dales.

AYSGARTH FALLS

STARTING AND FINISHING
POINT
Aysgarth Falls car-park and National
Park Centre (98-012888). Travelling
from Hawes along the A684 turn L
about ½ mile (800 m) after Aysgarth,
the car-park is on the L soon after a
bridge.
LENGTH
Upper Falls: ¾ mile (1.2 km). Middle
and Lower Falls: 3 miles (5 km)
ASCENT
Upper Falls: 50 feet (15 m). Middle
and Lower Falls: 100 feet (30 m)

After Malham and Bolton Abbey the falls at Aysgarth probably
attract more visitors than any other place within the National
Park. Due to the difficulties of crossing the river it is probably
better to visit the Upper Falls separately. The longer walk to the
Middle and Lower Falls can be extended to Castle Bolton if time
is available.

ROUTE DESCRIPTION (Map 2)

Upper Falls: Leave the car-park at the opposite end from the
road on a path which descends to the L. By the bridge and road
go through a small gate and walk up-stream along a pleasant
grassy bank as far as a fence. Return by the same route. The best
view of the Upper Falls can be obtained from the road bridge
(1) (2).

Middle and Lower Falls: Walk from the car-park into the
road and turn R. Where the road bends R go L along a path (PFS
'Middle Force/Lower Force'). The Middle Falls can best be seen
from the viewing platform at the side of the path. For the

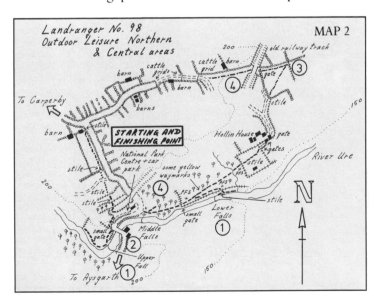

Lower Falls, continue along the path to the L of the river through a wood eventually reaching a small gate; beyond continue to a gate where a descent can be made down a path on the R to the river. The Lower Falls are nearby *(1)*.

After viewing, return to the stile and start to walk back towards the small gate. About half-way along at a PFS ('Aysgarth/Castle Bolton') turn back half R and follow a footpath (marked by yellow waymarks) to a stile. Cross the next field to a gate and then on to the farm just ahead (Hollin House). Go through a stile by a gate to the L of a building and follow the farm road through the farm. Go through the gate by the last building and about 100 yards (90 m) later branch half R at a junction to follow a fence. At a wall go over a stile and continue in approximately the same direction *(3)* to the far corner of the field.

Do *not* go through the gate in the corner but turn back half L and follow the wall *(4)* — i.e. the boundary of the field. Eventually reach a road and follow this — later between walls — to a junction. Go L and after about 50 yards (45 m) turn R over a stile. Follow the wall on the L (i.e. alongside the road) to another stile. Continue in the same direction, descending, as the wall swings away, to a further stile by a gate, then on through yet another stile and then a small gate. Finally, go down some steps into the car-park *(4)*.

1 *The Aysgarth Falls*
   The Falls are caused by resistant limestone beds of the Yoredale Series (see page 16) outcropping in the floor of the valley through which the River Ure flows. Wensleydale is named, not after the main river which flows through it as with other Dales, but from the village of Wensley some miles downstream. In the Yorkshire Dales the term 'pot-hole' has become synonymous with cave systems containing vertical pitches, but it is more correctly applied to round holes produced in stream beds by stones swirled around in the current. The flat rock beds below the Lower Falls at Aysgarth contain some fine examples.

2 *Yore Mill*
   The large building by the bridge at Aysgarth is Yore Mill, built in the nineteenth century on the remains of an earlier mill damaged by fire. It is now the premises of the Yorkshire Museum of Carriages and Horse Drawn Vehicles.

3 *Bolton Castle*
   The large and spectacular castle seen directly ahead as you

The Lower Falls at Aysgarth

cross the fields from Hollin House is Bolton Castle. Built between 1375 and 1399, in a period of intense castle-building brought about by threat of invasion from French and Scots, by Richard Lord Scrope, Chancellor to Richard II, it is regarded as one of the finest extant examples of a courtyard castle. The extent of its interior layout clearly indicates that it was built as a spacious residence as well as for defensive purposes. The central courtyard is formed by a high curtain wall linking four rectangular towers each nearly 100 feet (30 m) high; two smaller towers are placed midway on the north and south sides. The curtain wall is three stories high and the main towers five stories, giving a total of about 70 rooms.

Mary, Queen of Scots was imprisoned there for six months from July, 1568 before being moved to Tutbury Castle in Staffordshire; during the Civil War it was besieged for more than a year by Parliamentary forces before surrender. Partly dismantled after the Civil War it has since been somewhat restored and is open to the public.

4   *The Leyburn-Hawes railway*

The disused railway track crossed on the return leg of the route was a branch line from Leyburn (reached by railway in 1855) to Hawes where it connected with a branch of the Settle–Carlisle railway operated by the Midland Railway Company. The line was constructed by the North Eastern Railway Company and opened for traffic as far as Hawes in 1878. It served the northern dales for many years for the carrying of quarry stone, dairy products such as milk, butter and cheese, tourists and even war supplies during the two World Wars. There were five stations: Wensley, Redmire, Aysgarth, Askrigg and Hawes. All these stations were closed to passenger traffic in 1954 and the last three to goods in 1964. The metals westwards from Redmire were lifted and the station properties disposed of, but the line to Redmire retained for the use of the Redmire Limestone Quarry Company.

The old line is private property except at Aysgarth where a section of the line can be visited. The cafeteria, toilets and house by the National Park Centre were railway cottages and the disused railway station can be seen across the bridge. The entrance to the track is up the steps directly across the car-park from the National Park Centre.

1·3

CAUTLEY SPOUT

STARTING AND FINISHING POINT

Cross Keys Temperance Hotel, 4½ miles (7.5 km) from Sedbergh on the A683 to Kirkby Stephen (98-698969). A few cars may be parked in the small lay-by above the footbridge at the start of the walk

LENGTH

2½ miles (4 km)

ASCENT

500 feet (150 m)

Cautley Spout, on the eastern flank of the Howgills overlooking the Rawthey valley, is one of the most spectacular waterfalls in the National Park. A magnificent cascade of white water hundreds of feet long, its visual impact is heightened considerably by its position at the centre of a huge valley of rock and scree. It is easily and quickly reached from the Cross Keys Hotel on the Sedbergh–Kirkby Stephen road by a pleasant path which follows the north bank of Cautley Holme Beck. The only climbing (which can be omitted) takes place towards the end where the path rises to a viewpoint above the Spout.

ROUTE DESCRIPTION (Map 3)

Descend to the footbridge and cross to the opposite bank of the

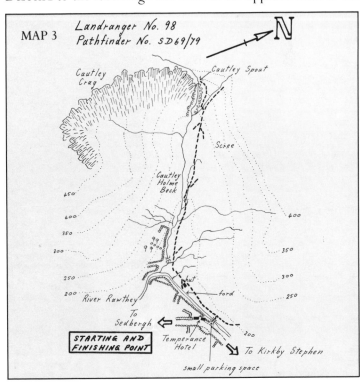

37

The Cross Keys Temperance Hotel. The walk goes up the valley behind the hotel.

stream. There turn L and follow a path going downstream on the R bank. Pass a small hut and soon afterwards at a stream junction turn R. Follow the path to the R of the subsidiary stream (the Spout is now obvious on the hillside ahead) crossing a large mound in the base of the valley and finally rising to a good viewpoint at the top of the main fall. Return by the same route. Care should be taken on the final rise by the Spout where the drop to the stream is considerable.

Cautley Crag and the Spout under winter snow

1·4

AROUND SEMER WATER

STARTING AND FINISHING
POINT
On the foreshore at the north-east
side of Semer Water, by the road
from Countersett to Stalling Busk,
where cars may be parked for a small
fee (pay at Low Blean Farm on the
walk if no one is in attendance)
(98-921876)
LENGTH
3¾ miles (6 km)
ASCENT
150 feet (45 m)

Unlike some other National Parks such as Snowdonia or the
Lake District, there are few lakes, natural or otherwise, within
the area of the Yorkshire Dales. But, of the few, Malham Tarn
and Semer Water are outstanding. This walk follows pleasant
field paths and farm lanes around Semer Water as far as Marsett;
a length of quiet road has to be walked on the return leg.

ROUTE DESCRIPTION (Map 4)

Turn R in the road and walk along it as far as a farm (Low Blean)

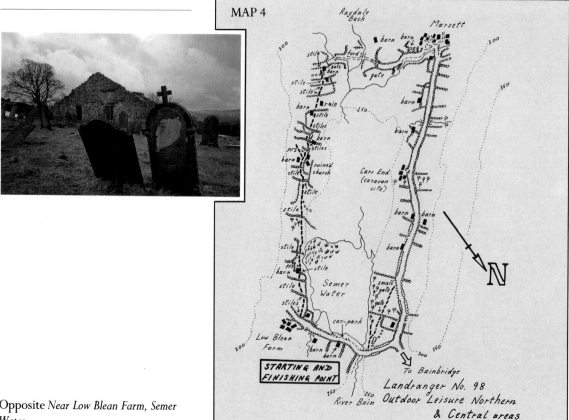

MAP 4

*Opposite Near Low Blean Farm, Semer
Water*

Semer Water

on the L, keeping the lake on your R (pay any parking fee at the farm). Immediately after the farm, where the road starts to climb, go R through a stile (PFS). Follow a clear footpath across three fields to a stile to the R of a barn. Beyond, continue on this path in the same direction leaving Semer Water behind to eventually pass to the L of a ruined church and churchyard.

From the church continue with the wall on your R; at a path junction taking the R-hand one (PFS 'Marsett') to a stile in a wall corner. The path then continues in the same general direction over nine fields to reach a farm lane to the L of a barn. Turn R and follow the lane to the village of Marsett.

At the road in Marsett turn R over the bridge and follow the road for about 1 mile (1.6 km). Where the road starts to descend steeply into a valley (Semer Water will be down to your R) go through a small gate to the R (PFS) a short distance down the hill. Take a path which goes down half L to a gate in a wall corner. Beyond the gate continue in the same direction across a pasture to reach a clear path, follow this to the road. Turn R for the parking place.

1·5

Clapham Beck to Ingleborough Cave

STARTING AND FINISHING
POINT
Clapham National Park Centre and
car-park (98-745692)
LENGTH
3½ miles (5.5 km)
ASCENT
500 feet (150 m)

A delightful walk through beautiful woods by Clapham Beck as far as Ingleborough Cave. The return is along a green lane on higher ground. Most of the route coincides with the National Park Nature Trail No. 3, described in a pamphlet obtainable from the Information Centre in Clapham.

Route Description (Map 5)

Leave the car-park past the National Park Centre and turn R in the road. After a few yards, cross the river over a delightful stone footbridge, turning R in the road on the opposite side. Walk up the road by the stream to a L-hand bend. Immediately after the bend turn R through a gate. You are now entering

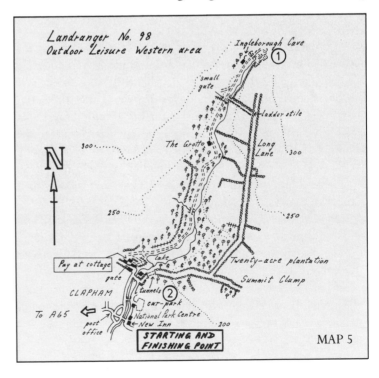

private grounds and a small payment must be made at the cottage directly ahead.

Turn R at the cottage and go along a clear path through a wall gap and then a small gate. The path bends back half L and then back half R (where a path comes in from the L), further along. Climb up a small hill to a junction of paths. Take the wide path to the L which goes along the L shore of the lake. No difficulty will now be found in following this very clear path through attractive woods. After about 1 mile (1.6 km) go through a small gate into open country. Continue along the path for a further 400 yards (370 m) to Ingleborough Cave *(1)*.

Return along the path back to the small gate. Do not go through but instead drop down L to a footbridge. Cross and climb up the field keeping a wall on your L. At the top cross a ladder stile into a walled lane. Turn R down the lane. Further along, the lane descends and then ascends again by a wood to a T-junction, here turn R. Follow the lane as it descends through two short tunnels *(2)* to reach the road by the church in Clapham. Turn L and walk down the road back to the car-park where you started the walk.

1 Ingleborough Cave

This is one of three show caves within the area of the National Park, the others being White Scar Cave on the B6255 road $2\frac{1}{2}$ miles (4 km) from Ingleton towards Hawes, and Stump Cross Caverns 4 miles (7.25 km) west of Pateley Bridge.

Prior to 1837 no more than about 70 feet (20 m) of the cave had been explored, as far as a stalagmite barrier and pool which barred further progress. In that year the barrier was broken down on the orders of the owner of that time thus draining the pool and allowing further exploration to be made. More recently cave-diving techniques have enabled the system to be still further extended to give a link with Gaping Gill (see page 85). The stream-opening a few yards from Ingleborough Cave is known as Beck Head and joins with it through a series of flooded sections.

Ingleborough Cave was first opened to tourists in 1838 and has continued to be popular ever since. Parties are guided underground for about $\frac{1}{3}$ mile (0.5 km) daily from March to October.

2 Ingleborough Hall

The large house on the west side of Clapham is Ingleborough Hall, home of the Farrer family for many years.

Clapham

Ingleborough Cave

Originally the building was a farmhouse, converted first into a shooting lodge and then into the Hall between 1820 and 1830. The two tunnels traversed on the return leg of the route were built over Thwaite Lane about the same time for the convenience of the occupants of the house and also to preserve the right of way. Clapham village itself was also considerably altered with the destruction of the vicarage and tithe barn, and the lake seen along the way formed by damming Clapham Beck. The church of St James was completely rebuilt in 1814 except for the tower.

Reginald John Farrer (1880–1920) was the most famous member of the family. Renowned as a botanist, writer and traveller he introduced many new plant species into the grounds of Ingleborough Hall and elsewhere. The specimens of *Carpinus turczaninowii* in the famous gardens at Highdown in West Sussex, for example, were raised from seed collected by Farrer in 1914. He died in 1920 in Burma.

The Hall is now a residential Outdoor Education Centre for the use of children from a number of Yorkshire Authority areas.

1·6

THE WATERFALLS WALK

STARTING AND FINISHING
POINT
Ingleton (98-695733)
LENGTH
4 miles (6.5 km)
ASCENT
550 feet (170 m)

The adjacent valleys of the Twiss and Doe to the north of Ingleton narrow in places to impressive gorges and hold high and magnificent waterfalls. The Waterfalls Walk (sometimes called the Ingleton Glens Walk) follows a circular route in the best of the two valleys. It is one of the most popular walks in the Dales, rightly regarded as a local classic. The walk follows the Twiss upstream to above Thornton Force, then crosses over to the Doe which is then followed downstream and back to Ingleton. The paths in the two valleys have been extensively re-surfaced giving them a somewhat artificial character. In no way does this detract from the route however, for it is superb throughout and few others — if any — can match it for sustained interest. At some points the path is unfenced and runs above considerable drops; care is therefore essential, particularly with children. A small charge is made for admission.

ROUTE DESCRIPTION (Map 6)

From the church in Ingleton take the road which drops down steeply to a bridge. Continue along the road soon crossing a second bridge. (The two rivers crossed by the bridges are the Doe and Twiss respectively which meet a short distance to the south-west.) Immediately after the second bridge, where the road bends L, go R through a gate. Pass the café to a small hut, just before the old railway embankment *(1)*.

Continue ahead through the gap in the embankment and cross the car-park to the far end. From there, follow the clear path which leads through small gates along the gorge of Swilla Glen and through lovely woods, keeping to the L of the river throughout. After about $\frac{3}{4}$ mile (1.2 km) cross the stream over a footbridge (Manor Bridge) and continue along the opposite bank of the stream, to re-cross after a bend by a second footbridge (Pecca Bridge). Just ahead of this footbridge are the first waterfalls (Pecca Falls) set in spectacular rock-scenery. The path

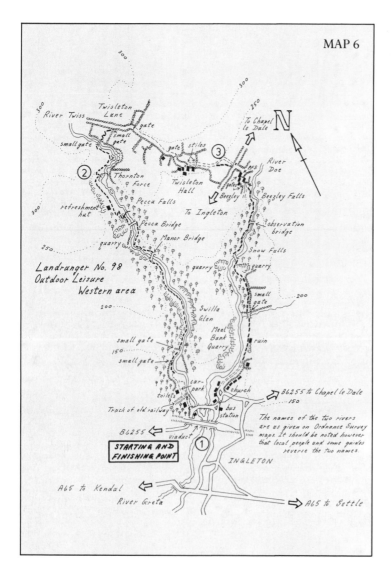

MAP 6

continues on the L bank up steep steps past Pecca Falls and a refreshment hut to a further waterfall, Thornton Force *(2)*. This is by far the largest and most interesting of the waterfalls along the route. Continue past the Force to a third footbridge (Ravenray Bridge).

Cross and climb the steps ahead up the hill to a small gate in the top R-hand corner of the field. In the walled lane beyond (Twisleton Lane) turn R and follow it to a farm (Twisleton Hall). Go past barns and through the stile by a gate to the L of the house. Follow the farm road through a further stile and down to a road *(3)*. Take the lane opposite, soon turning R in front of a

Thornton Force

farmhouse (Beezley Farm — refreshments). Go past the farm-house to a gate and along the farm road to a second gate. Immediately after the second gate turn down L to reach a river (the Doe) by a waterfall (Beezley Falls).

Follow downstream on the very obvious path keeping to the R bank. As a spectacle this is easily the most impressive part of the route, for the path follows a deep ravine past white falls, brown watershoots and dark, sinister pools of deep water. In one place an observation bridge has been erected across the gorge to give a breathtaking and unforgettable view of the ravine at its most savage point.

Much lower down, cross over a second footbridge to the opposite bank and follow the path as it leaves the stream to the L. Continue along the obvious path past a quarry and through woods to a small gate, then beyond over more open ground to a road. Follow this back to Ingleton.

1 *Railways at Ingleton*

The large viaduct crossing the Greta to the south-west of the village centre carried the now disused railway line over the river, the old railway station being at the south-eastern end. The embankment immediately after the small hut at the entrance to the Waterfalls Walk carried a branch line from the main track to Mealbank Quarry which is passed towards the end of the walk.

2 *Thornton Force*

The Pecca Falls are a series of magnificent cascades, Thornton Force by comparison is a mad torrent of white water falling in one tremendous leap into a plunge pool below. Its open situation, directly opposite the footpath as it curves to the right above the small refreshment hut, is ideal, for the Force is both a spectacle and one of the most interesting and well-known geological features in Britain. It is also a place to stir the imagination. The upper part of the rock-face of the fall is of grey, horizontal limestone, the lowest part of vertical and greenish Ingleton slates. Separating the two is a thin conglomerate of smoothly rounded pebbles cemented together. It is the site of an ancient pebble beach over which the sea washed some time between 350 and 500 million years ago. Later the beach was covered by shallow seas and deposited organic remains formed the overlying limestone layer. The junction of the limestone and slate is called an unconformity — the rocks above were not laid down in succession to those below, but instead there is a gap in the time scale of origin caused by the erosion of intervening layers of rock.

3 *Skirwith Quarry*
    The large quarry, seen across the Doe Valley as you descend
    towards it, is Skirwith Quarry worked for gritstone by Amey
    Roadstone Company, a member of the Gold Fields Group.
    The rock, which is very hard and abrasion resistant, is used as
    a road surface aggregate and railway ballast.

The Twiss below Manor Bridge

1·7

TO HARDRAW FORCE

STARTING AND FINISHING POINT
The National Park Centre and car-park at Hawes (98-876899)
LENGTH
4¾ miles (7.5 km)
ASCENT
350 feet (110 m)

Hardraw Force is the highest unbroken fall in Britain; much less well-known or visited are the upper falls set in sylvan woods. This walk is unique in that it includes a compulsory traverse of The Green Dragon public house. Not surprisingly, it is one of the most popular walks within the Park.

ROUTE DESCRIPTION (Map 7)

Go on to the old platform (1) behind the National Park Centre and cross the track at the bridge end. Turn R along the far platform and then L up to the road. There turn R. About 100 yards (90 m) from the bridge go L through a small gate and

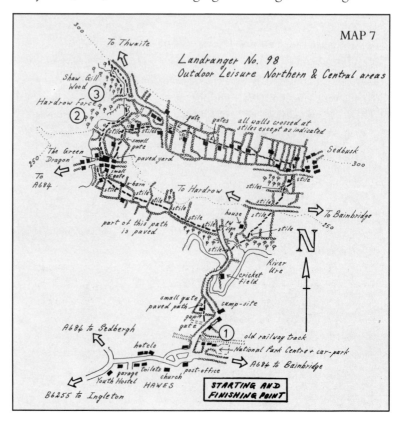

54

Old Bridge near the Ure. Hawes can be seen in the distance.

follow a paved path through two fields to rejoin the road further along. Turn L over a bridge and past a small cricket field. When the road starts to climb, immediately after a belt of trees, go L up some steps and through a stile (PW sign). Follow the path by the wall along the bottom edge of the field. Little or no difficulty should now be found in following the clear path (much of it paved) which goes in an almost straight line through a series of stiles to Hardraw. Reach the road opposite the church and The Green Dragon.

Hardraw Force *(2)* can only be reached through The Green Dragon on payment of a small fee. From the rear of the public house go along a path to the R of the river. After viewing, return to the front of the public house.

Leave Hardraw down the R-hand side of the public house through the small paved yard of a cottage. Climb up the field beyond to a small gate and up the next field to a stile L of a house (West House). In front of the house turn L and follow the farm road as far as a road, there turn L. Where the road bends R go straight ahead down a walled path to a footbridge *(3)*. Cross and follow the stream on its L bank past several small falls to a further footbridge. Cross and return on the opposite side back to West House.

Back at the house turn L between the house and a barn and follow a path to a stile to the R of a further barn. Cross the next field to enter a lane. Turn R to road, there turn L. After 25 yards (23 m) turn R over a stile. Go half L to a farm road and gate and beyond by a large barn leave the farm road half L again to a further stile. The path goes in a straight line over a number of stiles and gates (on my count thirteen!) towards Sedbusk.

In the last but one field before the village, turn R immediately after the stile along a path to a stile in the far corner. This leads into a road. Cross the road half R to another stile and descend the field beyond past a barn to a lower stile. Continue in the same general direction over two further fields to reach a lower road. Again, cross to a stile opposite and descend past a house to the bottom R-hand corner of the field. Continue to descend over an old bridge and into a road. Turn L and retrace your steps back to Hawes.

1 The Wensleydale Railway

The station at Hawes was built as a joint station between the Midland Railway Company's branch line from Garsdale (then called Hawes Junction) and that of the North Eastern Railway Company's line from Leyburn, the linkage being completed in 1878. It remained open until 1964 when the entire line between Garsdale and Redmire was closed. The state of the station buildings, platforms and trackway rapidly deteriorated, and it was fortunate that they were taken over by the National Park Authority. The main station building is now used as a National Park Centre, the goods warehouse and office have become the Upper Dales Folk Museum and the station yard is a car-park, whilst the waiting room on the far platform is a warden's workshop. The house to the left of the car-park entrance was the Station Master's residence.

2 Hardraw Force

The slopes of Wensleydale are characterized by near-horizontal banks of relatively hard-wearing limestone of the Yoredale Series which produce superb waterfalls where side streams flow over them. The Force at Hardraw was produced in this way by the water of a beck flowing over a limestone scar resting upon softer shales. The light-grey horizontal bands of limestone are obvious as are the much darker shales at their base. In the course of time the stream has eroded back considerably into the hillside to produce the ravine, and

Hardraw Force

the greater erosion of the shales has formed a bank under the overhangs of limestone.

The thunder of the Force can be heard long before you reach it, but a sight of the fall is delayed until the final yards. Even so, the great drop of brownish water nearly 100 feet (30 m) high set in its amphitheatre of high cliffs is extremely impressive; the cloak of trees removing from the scene that bareness and austerity that is characteristic of Gordale.

The gorge was the scene during the nineteenth century and again in the 1920s for brass band contests and the old bandstand can be seen on the left just after the footbridge; on the hillside opposite are the tiers cut for spectators. These contests were revived recently, but have now been discontinued once more.

3 *Shaw Gill Wood*

Above the Force, this is largely neglected compared with the Force itself, but it is a delight not to be missed if a few extra minutes can be found for a diversion away from the main route. Neither of the two main waterfalls approaches the Force as a spectacle, but their setting is much superior.

In the Yorkshire Dales National Park, as elsewhere, teams of public-spirited people — mainly young people — have given up much of their free time so that the countryside should be the pleasanter for others. Duke of Edinburgh Award Scheme Volunteers assisted in the restoration of the paths at Shaw Gill in August, 1980 and the top footbridge was built by the Army Apprentices College, Chepstow, in October, 1979.

1·8

UPPER WHARFEDALE

STARTING AND FINISHING
POINT
Buckden car-park (98-942774)
LENGTH
4¾ miles (7.5 km)
ASCENT
500 feet (150 km)

Buckden, Cray and Hubberholme form a compact group of villages in Upper Wharfedale which are linked together in this short circular walk. It is probably best done in an anti-clockwise direction so that the climbs are gradual. The paths from Buckden to Cray and on to Scar House above Hubberholme are high on the hillside giving magnificent views over the Dale. The way back to Buckden is by the river and uses a section of the Dales Way, a long-distance footpath from Ilkley to Bowness-on-Windermere.

ROUTE DESCRIPTION (Map 8)

Leave the car-park at Buckden through a gate at the opposite end from the toilet block (there is a PFS 'Buckden Pike/Cray High Bridge' by the gate). Follow the clear path which climbs slowly up the hillside. Above a wood (on your L) reach a gate and continue with a wall on your L through two further gates. Shortly afterwards, where the wall bends L, continue in the same direction to another gate. 60 yards (55 m) after this turn L through a small gate in the wall (PFS 'Buckden/Cray/Cray Bridge') and follow a path down the hillside to the small hamlet of Cray, crossing a ford to reach the road near the White Lion Inn.

Cross the road and go up the farm road to the R of the inn. At the rear of the inn take the R-fork at a junction and rise to a gate to the R of a barn. Go through a gate to the R of the next barn, and continue along a lane between walls to a third gate to the R of still another barn. Follow the farm road through two more gates. Cross the field beyond to a gate L of a barn and then bend R following a wall to a footbridge.

Continue half L from the footbridge and then along the top of a small scar with beautiful views of Wharfedale over to the L. (There is no footpath along this section, but the route is indicated by occasional yellow waymarks.) Cross a gap in a wall about 25 yards (23 m) R of the far L-hand corner of the field; then continue in the same direction keeping a wall on your L to

59

Buckden and Upper Wharfedale

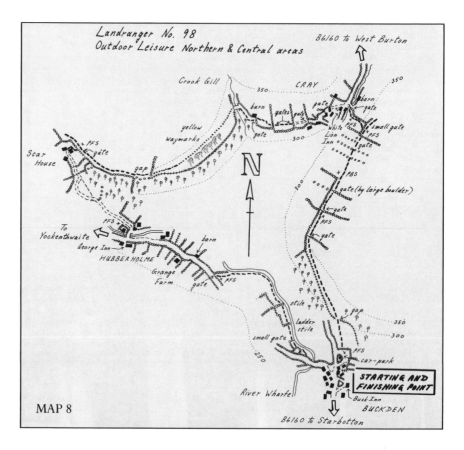

Landranger No. 98
Outdoor Leisure Northern & Central areas

MAP 8

reach the farm of Scar House. By the farm at a PFS drop down to a gate on the L. Bend R then L around the R-hand side of the farmhouse to the farm road. Follow the farm road down to eventually reach the road by the church at Hubberholme (if you have a few minutes to spare, visit this charming Dales church which has a rare rood loft dated 1558 and a superb Norman arch).

Cross the bridge and turn L in front of the inn. Follow the road past a large house on your R (Grange Farm) and a barn on your L. At the end of the next field on the L after the barn go through a gate on the L (PFS 'Buckden Bridge'). Follow the path with a wall on your L to the river and then along the river bank to eventually rejoin the road. Turn L over the bridge back to Buckden and the car-park.

Opposite *Hubberholme Church: rood loft*

1·9

GORDALE SCAR AND MALHAM COVE

STARTING AND FINISHING POINT
Malham National Park Centre car-park (98-900627)
LENGTH
4¾ miles (7.5 km)
ASCENT
650 feet (200 m)

Gordale Scar, a magnificent ravine with overhanging walls 150 feet (45 m) high, is rivalled only by Malham Cove as the most impressive sight in the Yorkshire Dales. This route includes both. Waymarks have been placed throughout. A short and easy but superb walk in magnificent limestone country. Janet's Foss and Little Gordale, also on the route, would be worth a visit on their own account, but on this route are dwarfed in comparison with the Cove and Scar.

ROUTE DESCRIPTION (Map 9)

Leave the car-park in Malham *(1)* and turn L down a minor road

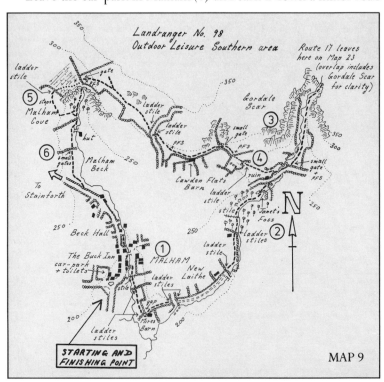

Opposite Gordale Scar

past the Information Centre. At the road turn L again. Opposite Sparth House, which is just before the Buck Inn, turn R and cross the stream over a small footbridge. On the far side turn R and walk downstream. Soon, cross a stile and then follow the path across two fields to reach a ladder stile in a wall corner. Immediately after the ladder stile bend L with the wall and go through a gap just before a barn. Follow the wall (which is now on your R), soon crossing a ladder stile into a lane.

Go ahead for 25 yards (23 m) to a further ladder stile. Cross and follow the clear path by a wall to reach still another ladder stile just past a barn. Beyond, follow the path to the L of a stream, then follow a wall to twin ladder stiles, and finally continue on through a beautiful ravine (Little Gordale) to reach a waterfall, Janet's Foss *(2)*. The path goes up to the L to a road.

Turn R along the road. Immediately after a bridge and bend in the road go L through a small gate. The way ahead is now obvious, along a very clear path as far as the lower waterfall within the great ravine of Gordale Scar *(3)*. Do not attempt to go further up the ravine, but instead retrace your route back to the road and turn R. After the bend go R over the old bridge and immediately R again over a ladder stile.

Go half L to a wall corner and climb the hill ahead keeping by the wall. At the top *(4)* cross a ladder stile and go half R to a second ladder stile. Here, turn L on a grassy path keeping the wall on your L. Pass through a small gate (notice the dry valley to the R) and keep in the same direction with the wall. After a barn where the wall bends L leave the wall to continue in the same direction across open ground to reach a road.

Cross the road, go over the ladder stile opposite and along a path half R which leaves the walls to L and R. Eventually you will reach the wall again on your L at a corner where the path forks. Take the L fork which descends to a gate in a wall. The edge of the Malham Cove precipice *(5)* will now be obvious a short distance to your L. (This edge is not fenced and should be approached with great care.)

Cross the limestone pavements keeping well to the R of the cliff edge to reach a ladder stile on the far side. Cross and descend L on a clear path. Lower down below the cliff turn L with the path heading directly towards the stream. Near to the stream the path bends to the R. (It is worthwhile making a short detour here to the L to the foot of the Cove where the stream emerges.) Follow the path keeping to the R side of the stream to eventually reach a road *(6)*. Turn L and follow the road back to Malham. Or better still, go L over the stile from the road immediately after Beck Hall and follow a secluded footpath on the R bank of the stream back to the centre of the village.

1 Malham See page 30.

2 Janet's Foss

The small but delightful waterfall of Janet's Foss, and the wooded limestone gorge of 'Little Gordale', make a fitting introduction to the much greater glories of the Scar itself. 'Foss' is an old Norse word for waterfall whilst Janet was reputedly the queen of the local fairies who lived in the cave behind the fall. The original rock face responsible for the waterfall now lies behind a screen of tufa, a soft porous limestone, built over it by the stream. A good time to visit the Foss is mid-May when the floor of the ravine is covered with a carpet of wild garlic.

3 Gordale Scar

Arguably the two most spectacular sights in the Yorkshire Dales—Malham Cove and Gordale Scar— lie near to each other within one mile of Malham village, both formed in a similar manner by stream erosion back into the scarp of the Middle Craven Fault. But there the similarity ends. The glories of the Cove are an obvious feature before you as you approach along Malham Beck. The glories of Gordale by contrast are hidden away, to be revealed only at the last moment when the walker turns the corner into the extremity of the gorge. The huge overhanging walls of Great Scar Limestone, the deep shadow, the chill and the menace of the great ravine of Gordale impress all who go there.

It is likely that the ravine is a collapsed cave system, the stream originally disappearing down a swallow hole on the moor beyond. The rock step by the lower fall, which is climbed on Route 17, was once extensively covered with tufa, although this is now being rapidly worn away.

Some very hard rock-climbing has been seen upon the walls of Gordale. The first major route completed was the West Face Route in 1954 by D. Farley and N. Rhodes; this is a very severe route of 220 feet (70 m) which goes up the right wall of the ravine just above the lower waterfall. There are now about 130 routes on the Scar covering all the main faces.

4 Lynchets

An obvious feature of the Malham area, particularly to the east and west of Malham Beck, are the series of giant terraces or steps, each 100–200 yards (90–180 m) long, cut into and across the hillsides. They are called lynchets, a feature to be found both in other parts of the Dales and outside it in areas such as Cambridgeshire and Dorset. The ones in the Malham area were cut by Anglian farmers in the eighth century to produce the extra food needed by the growing villages, when the more suitable land in the valleys had been fully exploited.

The terraces, made by clearing and then levelling the ground, were essential for the teams of oxen used in ploughing which otherwise were unmanageable on steep hill slopes.

5 *Malham Cove* See page 30
6 *Iron-age field boundaries* See page 32

Malham Cove

Bolton Abbey and the Strid

STARTING AND FINISHING POINT
Bolton Abbey car-park (104-071539)
LENGTH
6½ miles (10.5 km)
ASCENT
100 feet (30 m)

Bolton Abbey and Bolton Woods are extremely popular in the summer months. The best time for this walk therefore is out-of-season when the crowds are elsewhere. The ruins and chapel of Bolton Abbey, beautiful woods and the impressive Strid are the main attractions along a particularly lovely stretch of the Wharfe. A straightforward walk, with virtually no climbing, which barely makes the moderate category. Bolton Woods is a conservation area, so please keep to the footpaths. A small fee should be paid on leaving the woods by the Cavendish Pavilion on the return route.

ROUTE DESCRIPTION (Map 10)

Leave the car-park to the R of the toilet block and village hall and walk along the minor road to a junction. Cross the road half L and go through the small gate in the gap in the high wall on the opposite side (sign 'To the Priory'). Follow the path beyond down to a footbridge over the river. On the far bank turn L and after a few yards go R up some steps at a path junction. Follow the path for ⅔ mile (1.1 km) to a road.

Go L along the road, soon crossing a ford over a footbridge. Immediately after the ford take the path on the L going R over a stile to follow a path on the R bank of the river. Cross a minor road by a bridge (refreshments are available at the Cavendish Pavilion on the opposite bank) and continue along the path on the R bank of the stream, soon reaching a road. Go L along the road, over a small bridge and then leave it to the L again after a few yards to continue in the same direction along a footpath. Follow this footpath alongside the river to reach the Strid *(1)*. Care should be taken on this section as some scrambling is required. Beyond, continue on the R bank, rising R to a stile after ½ mile (800 m). Follow the path to an aqueduct *(2)* over the river, and cross this to the opposite bank.

Turn L along the path by the river and walk downstream,

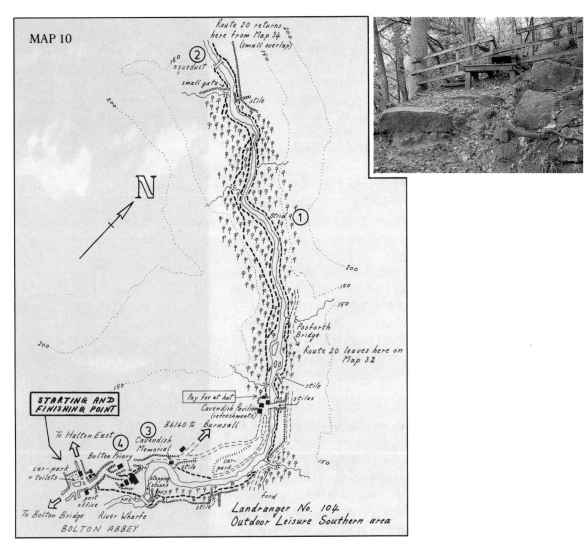

soon re-entering the woods at a small gate. Follow the clear path through the woods above the river to reach the Cavendish Pavilion again after 1½ miles (2.5 km); there is a choice of routes along this section, either low down by the river or higher up the hillside. As the woods are private property and contain a number of nature trails, in spring and summer a small entrance fee must be paid at the small hut on leaving the woods.

Continue past the Pavilion and by the river to the far end of the large parking/picnic area. At the end, take a path which goes half R across open ground rising at the end to a stile and road. Turn L along the road past a fountain *(3)* — there are lovely views down to the L over the river and the Priory. After 300 yards (275 m) where the road bends R go L through a small gate. Pass to the R of the Priory church *(4)* and then along the drive curving R to the road. Turn L for the car-park.

1 The Strid

At the Strid, the Wharfe, which shortly before was up to 60 feet (18 m) wide, is forced through a narrow rock ravine barely 6–8 feet (2–2½ m). The result is a mad frenzy of white water rushing and sliding its way through the gap into sinister black pools below. The rocks on each side are smoothed and rounded by the action of the water, and just near enough to tempt. Attempts to jump the Strid have however cost a few people their lives.

2 The Aqueduct

The aqueduct crossing the Wharfe just south of Barden Bridge carries water from the reservoirs in Nidderdale to Bradford.

3 The Cavendish Memorial Fountain

The tall structure on the roadside at the top of the entrance to the Cavendish Pavilion car-park is a covered fountain erected by the electors of the West Riding as a tribute to the memory of Frederick Charles Cavendish (born 30 November, 1836. Died 6 May, 1882.) A further memorial in the form of a cross, erected by the tenantry of the Bolton Abbey estates, is in the churchyard.

Frederick Charles Cavendish, son of the 7th Duke of Devonshire, was appointed Chief Secretary for Ireland by Gladstone in 1882. On 6 May, only a few hours after his arrival in Ireland, he was stabbed to death with his undersecretary T. H. Burke while walking in Phoenix Park, Dublin. The assassins were a group of Irish extremists known as the Invincibles. It appears that Burke was the actual target, Cavendish being killed while trying to defend him against his attackers. The murder effectively stopped any attempts to solve the Irish problem for several years.

4 Bolton Priory

In 1120 a Priory of Augustinian Canons (Black Canons) was founded at Embsay about 4 miles (6.5 km) to the west of Bolton Abbey. This was moved in 1151 to the present — and much more attractive — site by Alicia de Romilly whose parents had established the original Priory at Embsay. The church and some domestic buildings for the Canons were built in the twelfth century, with further building in the fourteenth, considerably extending the size of the Priory. Work on the West Tower was begun in 1520 but never completed, the Dissolution reaching the Priory in 1539. The Nave of the church was spared and is now used as the Priory

Bolton Priory

Bolton Woods

Church of Bolton Abbey, with the chancel and transepts forming impressive ruins behind. Recently, a national appeal exceeded expectations by raising £400,000 for essential repair and restoration work on this church which attracts some 200,000 visitors from all corners of the earth each year. The work included the roofing of the West Tower.

The beautiful hall facing the west doorway of the church is Bolton Hall, a private residence of the Duke of Devonshire. The square centre tower is the old gateway of the Priory which was left intact at the Dissolution. The south wing was added in 1720 and the north wing in 1843.

The Old Rectory to the south of the Priory ruins was built in 1700 as the result of a bequest by Robert Boyle to his nephew, Charles, Earl of Burlington, of a sum of money to be used for charitable purposes. The building was used as a school and as a house for the headmaster until 1874, when it became the rectory which it remained until 1978. An inscribed (in Latin) stone on the building describes the bequest. Robert Boyle is much better known for his scientific achievements and in particular for 'Boyle's Law' which was named after him.

HAWKSWICK MOOR

STARTING AND FINISHING
POINT
Kettlewell car-park (98-968722)
LENGTH
6¼ miles (10 km)
ASCENT
1500 feet (460 m)

The great ridge separating Littondale and Wharfedale is crossed by several excellent footpaths, all of them well-waymarked for the maintenance of inter-dale routes is high on the list of priorities of the National Park·Authority. The footpaths over Hawkswick Moor, near to the junction of the two Dales, are the shortest of these but, as might be expected, give the finest views. This walk is very popular and, as a result, the footpaths over the moor are now clear and should be easily followed. The route also includes a nice section between Hawkswick and Arncliffe by the river Skirfare.

ROUTE DESCRIPTION (Map 11)

Leave the car-park into the road and turn R over the bridge crossing the Wharfe. Walk along the road for 400 yards (365 m) then turn R through a gate (PFS 'Hawkswick'). At a path fork after 40 yards (35 m) go R and continue to rise soon reaching a small gate. Beyond, continue up by a wall to the L of a small ruin, bending R to a ladder stile opposite some trees just after a gap. From the stile the path rises, passing a crag and across the moor (there are yellow waymarks on this section). Continue along the edge of the moor; at the end the path swings half R to a ladder stile on the crest of the ridge. Follow the path on the far side, swinging R at a cairn, and start to descend towards Hawkswick. During the descent, reach a wall on the L and follow this to a gate. Beyond, continue to descend on a good grassy path with a wall to the L, bending L at the bottom into a lane. Follow the lane to a road and, there, bear L to a bridge (Hawkswick).

Cross the bridge and turn R along a lane by the river. By some farm buildings turn R down a narrow lane to a bridge. Do not cross the bridge, but go L over a ladder stile (PFS 'Arncliffe'). Continue on the L-bank of the river over two stiles to reach a footbridge; beyond, cross a further field. Cross the large field following on a clear path to a ladder stile by the river on the far side (thus cutting across a large loop of the river). Go over the

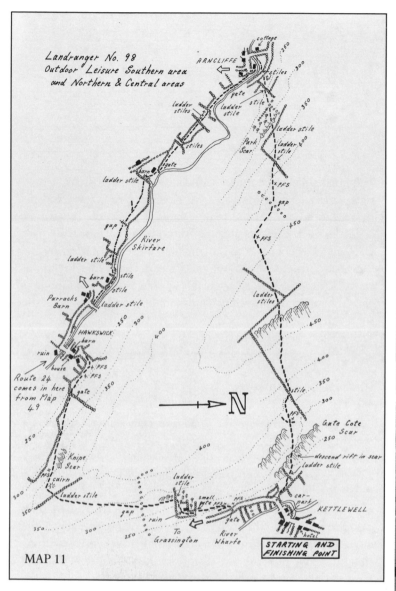

Landranger No. 98
Outdoor Leisure Southern area
and Northern & Central areas

MAP 11

footbridge ahead, then R of a barn to a gate. Turn half L across a field to cross the end of a lane by two stiles. Beyond, go to the R of a wall to a ladder stile and then across a field to rejoin the river at a further stile. Follow the path on the L bank of the river to Arncliffe; there go to the R of a large house to a gate in front of a ruin. Cross and turn L along a drive passing the church to a road.

Turn R in the road and walk to a bridge over the river. Cross and immediately turn R through a stile. Follow the stream to a

Arncliffe, Littondale

Old Cote Little Moor

road. Go over the stile on the opposite side and take the path which climbs half R to a ladder stile. Continue up the hill on the path to cross a further stile in a fence. 350 yards (320 m) higher on the path, climb a short face of rock and go over the ladder stile at the top. The path continues to ascend half R crossing two walls at ladder stiles (public footpath signs have been placed at two points where the path bends).

Finally, cross a wall on the ridge top at still another ladder stile and start to descend in the same direction, crossing a wall to the R by a stile after almost $\frac{1}{2}$ mile (800 m) — do not use the gate in the wall passed earlier. Descend in the same direction to cross a crag down a rift (yellow waymarks) and later a wall. Finally, reach the road by the bridge in Kettlewell and turn L for the car-park.

The Ascent of Pen-y-ghent

STARTING AND FINISHING
POINT
Horton in Ribblesdale car-park
(98-808726)
LENGTH
6½ miles (10.5 km)
ASCENT
1550 feet (470 m)

After Ingleborough, Pen-y-ghent is the most popular mountain in the Dales. Some of this popularity is probably due to its fine name which has a challenging sound about it much in keeping with the mountain itself. Its finest aspect undoubtedly is from the south around Churn Milk Hole, where its bold shape is said to resemble a crouching lion, but it is an imposing sight from any direction. The ascent from Horton in Ribblesdale via Brackenbottom and the subsequent descent via Hunt and Hull Pots is a magnificent walk, although a great deal of work has had to be done on it in order to combat the effect of erosion caused by the number of walkers.

Route Description (Map 12)

Walk from the car-park into the road and turn R. Continue along the road for 700 yards (640 m) to turn L by the village church and cross a bridge. Immediately after the bridge turn L along a minor road; continue along this road to the small hamlet of Brackenbottom.

Immediately before the first building on the L (a barn) go through a gate (PFS 'Pen-y-ghent') and on to a second gate (i.e. the centre one of three gates). After this second gate turn L and go up the hill with a wall on the L. The path follows near to the wall in a long and steady climb up the western flank of the south ridge of Pen-y-ghent, crossing three walls at stiles, to eventually reach the ridge crest at a ladder stile. Cross and turn L to commence the final steep climb. Some scrambling can be enjoyed here, but the path avoids the worst of the rocks by detouring to the R. Above the rocks follow the path to the R of the wall across to the summit *(1)*.

At the summit, cross the ladder stile and descend half R on a broad path to reach the edge of a steep section (cairns). Here the path bends R to descend slowly along the edge. Lower down, below the start of a cliff on the R, the path bends back L

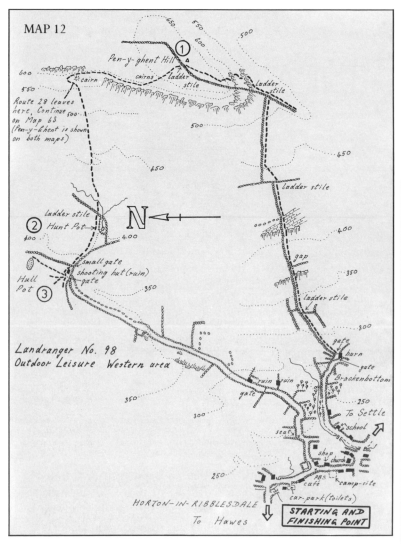

MAP 12

Pen-y-ghent Hill ①

cairn

cairns   ladder stile

ladder stile

600

550

Route 28 leaves here. Continue on Map 63 (Pen-y-ghent is shown on both maps)

500

450

450

ladder stile

500

400

ladder stile ②

Hunt Pot

400

N

small gate

shooting hut (ruin)

gate

Hull Pot ③

350

350

400

gap

350

ladder stile

Landranger No. 98
Outdoor Leisure Western area

300

gate

barn

gate

Brackenbottom

250

To Settle

school

ruin ruin

gate

seat

300

shop

church

250

P.B.S.

café   camp-site

car-park (toilets)

HORTON-IN-RIBBLESDALE

To Hawes

STARTING AND FINISHING POINT

by a large cairn. Go through the bend and then take the prominent path to the L descending the moor. Later cross a ladder stile, pass a pot-hole (Hunt Pot) *(2)*, and through a small gate to the end of a lane. (It is well worthwhile making a short detour here to see another famous pot-hole, Hull Pot *(3)*. At the lane end turn R and follow a path through a shallow valley for 350 yards (320 m). The pot-hole is very obvious. Afterwards return by the same route back to the lane end.) Go through the gate to enter the lane and follow this for 1⅔ miles (2.5 km) back to Horton in Ribblesdale. In the village turn R for the car-park (and the Pen-y-ghent café).

continued overleaf

Pen-y-ghent from near Hull Pot

1 Pen-y-ghent

The meaning of the name is still somewhat obscure, although it is Celtic in origin. Among the possibilities suggested are 'hill of the plain or open country' and 'hill of the winds'. The rock foundations are similar to those of Ingleborough: the flat top of the hill is formed by a cap, about 50 feet (15 m) thick, of Millstone Grit, underneath which are the Yoredale Series with Great Scar Limestone beginning at around 1300 feet (395 m). The characteristic 'stepped' appearance of Pen-y-ghent is due to the Millstone Grit and the beds of the Yoredale Series which have worn at different rates, so that the more resistant rocks now stand proud of the hillside. Potholes, caves and scars are characteristic features of the plateau formed by the limestone belt. Both Ingleborough and Pen-y-ghent are the remnants of a great rock plateau which originally covered the whole area around Ribblesdale. Rock climbing takes place on the gritstone edges of the mountain.

2 Hunt Pot

The sinister slit of Hunt Pot leads directly to a sheer drop of about 90 feet (27 m) followed by a second drop of about 70 feet (21 m). It was first descended in 1898.

3 Hull Pot

The opening of Hull Pot is enormous, about 185 feet × 45 feet (56 × 14 m). A stream bed reaches the lip of the pot on the north side, but water only flows over this in wet weather; more usually the stream sinks underground a short distance away to emerge as a waterfall from an opening below the old bed. The water then sinks immediately into the bed of the pot to re-appear at Brants Gill Head north of Horton. In extremely wet conditions, when the outlet passages cannot cope with the excess flow, the floor of the pot becomes covered with water.

Pen-y-ghent from near Churn Milk Hole

The Ascent of
Ingleborough

STARTING POINT
Clapham National Park Centre
car-park (98-746692)
FINISHING POINT
Ingleton (98-696732)
LENGTH
6½ miles (10.5 km)
ASCENT
1850 feet (560 m)

Whernside at 2415 feet (736 m) is the highest mountain within the National Park, but Ingleborough, 43 feet (13 m) lower, is by far the most imposing. To visitors and residents alike Ingleborough is *the* mountain of the Dales. Arguably, the best ascent is from Clapham via Ingleborough Cave and Gaping Gill and the best descent by Crina Bottom to Ingleton, which has a good bus service back to Clapham, and these therefore are the routes described. But on Ingleborough all routes are good.

ROUTE DESCRIPTION (Maps 5, 13, 14 — see also page 45)

Follow Route 5 as far as Ingleborough Cave *(1)*. Continue along the track past the cave and over the bridge immediately afterwards to eventually reach the imposing ravine of Trow Gill. Continue through the Gill to the far end, leaving up a short and easy scramble between sheer rock walls. Beyond, follow a path keeping a wall to the L. After about ½ mile (800 m) — and 125 yards (115 m) after a pot-hole to the R of the path — cross a ladder stile on the L (note that this is not the first ladder stile on the L after Trow Gill).

Follow the path up the moor past several pot-holes to reach Gaping Gill *(2)* — it is extremely dangerous to approach the open shaft — and then up towards the rocky summit ahead (Little Ingleborough). The path is clear except for a short section just before Gaping Gill; some cairns have also been built in the upper parts. Beyond the minor summit continue along the ridge and follow the obvious path up a boulder slope to reach the R edge of the main summit plateau. At the top, the path bends L on to the plateau. Cross to the summit cairn *(3)*.

For the descent, continue beyond the summit in the same direction as you approached to reach a large cairn on the far edge of the plateau. The descent path will be seen down to the L. No difficulty in route-finding should now be found for the path is very clear as it goes straight down the slope, although

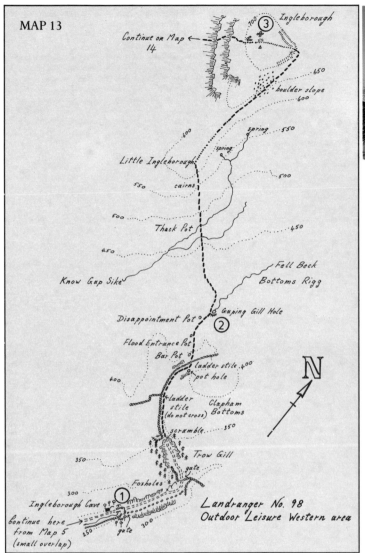

MAP 13

Continue on Map 14 ←

Ingleborough
③
700
650
boulder slope
600
spring
550
600
spring
Little Ingleborough
550
cairns
500
550
500
Thack Pot
450
450
Know Gap Sike
Fell Beck
Bottoms Rigg
Disappointment Pot
Gaping Gill Hole
②
Flood Entrance Pot
Bar Pot
ladder stile 400
pot hole
400
ladder stile (do not cross)
Clapham Bottoms
scramble 350
N
Trow Gill
350
gate
Foxholes
300
①
Ingleborough Cave
Landranger No. 98
Outdoor Leisure Western area
Continue here from Map 5 (small overlap)
250
gate
300

initially it is both steep and rough. Eventually, much lower down, pass a stream and water sinks on your L and the farm of Crina Bottom on your R. Soon after the farm reach the end of a green lane at a crossing wall and enter it over a ladder stile. Follow for about 1 mile (1.6 km); where it ends continue down over open ground on a footpath in the same general direction to reach a road. Turn L for the centre of Ingleton.

1 *Ingleborough Cave* See page 46
2 *Gaping Gill*

The great open shaft, 20 feet (6 m) in diameter, into which Fell Beck plunges, is the famous Gaping Gill.

It is apparent that Fell Beck once flowed through Trow

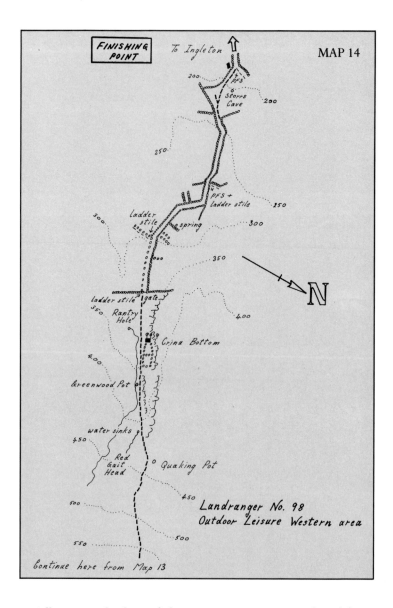

Gill to join the line of the present stream around Ingleborough Cave, for there are dry valleys both before and after Trow Gill which itself shows signs of water action. The dry pot-holes in the valley below Gaping Gill are the earlier sinks of Fell Beck; it is possible that in the future the flow of water into Gaping Gill will cease as a further pot-hole is opened higher up the hillside. The most convincing place to see all of this is on the final rise to the summit of Ingleborough from where, looking back, the valley of Fell Beck can be clearly seen down to and beyond Gaping Gill. Since the Gill was formed the stream has eroded deeply into the covering of boulder clay so that the valley above Gaping Gill is much deeper than that below it.

Opposite Crina Bottom *on the descent from Ingleborough*

The main shaft falls sheer for 340 feet (104 m), broken only by a ledge — Birkbeck's Ledge, named after an early explorer — at 190 feet (58 m), to the floor of a magnificent chamber 500 feet long by 90 feet wide and 110 feet high ($152 \times 27 \times 34$ m). The stream, falling down the shaft, disappears immediately into the floor of the chamber to emerge later at Beck Head Cave a few yards from Ingleborough Cave.

The first successful descent of Gaping Gill was made in August, 1895 by the French explorer, Edward Alfred Martel, the descent taking 23 minutes. Since then numerous expeditions into the Gill have extended the system to a total of about $6\frac{1}{2}$ miles (10.5 km) of passages and chambers, the most important of which have been named. It is thought highly unlikely however that the system is exhausted, with nothing further remaining for future explorers. Of particular interest for some time was a possible connection with Ingleborough Cave, for the furthest reaches of the Gaping Gill system — appropriately called The Far Country and The Far Waters — were within a few hundred feet of the known limit of the cave. This connection has now been achieved.

A winch is erected, by which the public may descend the main shaft, around the Spring and August Bank Holiday weekends. Information may be obtained from the National Park Centre at Clapham.

3 Ingleborough

The summit plateau of Ingleborough is particularly rich in remains from the past.

The entire summit, an area of about 15 acres (6 hectares) was originally enclosed by a single stone and rubble wall about 13 feet (4 m) thick made of millstone grit with an entrance probably to the south-west. Part of this wall was unfortunately destroyed in the construction of a summit cairn but much of it still remains. Within the wall many hut circles can be distinguished. The wall was probably built as a defensive position for times of trouble rather than as a centre of permanent occupation. It is the highest hillfort in England and Wales, probably of Iron Age origin, and it played an important part in the revolt of the Brigantes under Venutius against the Romans in the first century AD.

The cross-shaped wind shelter near to the Ordnance Survey obelisk was 'erected by the Ingleton Fell Rescue Team to Commemorate the Coronation of her Gracious Majesty Queen Elizabeth II, June 2nd, 1953'. At the centre and above eye-level is a direction indicator to local mountain summits.

On the eastern side, at the start of the descent to Ingleton,

are the remains of a tower built by Hornby Roughsedge, a mill-owner, about 1830 as a house of rest for visitors to the summit. It had a very short life, being damaged on the official opening day by some of the local participants, who were apparently somewhat the worse for drink. The damage was never repaired and the building soon fell into ruin.

The view back from the final rise to the summit of Ingleborough

2·14

UPPER SWALEDALE

STARTING AND FINISHING
POINT
Thwaite (98-892982). Leave cars
outside the village at some suitable
point.
LENGTH
8 miles (13 km)
ASCENT
900 feet (270 m)

Considered by many to be the finest of all the Yorkshire Dales,
Swaledale is remote and rugged with quiet villages of great
charm. Appropriately, the Pennine Way follows it for several
miles and another long-distance footpath, The Coast to Coast
Walk, crosses it at Keld. This very popular route links the
villages of Thwaite, Keld and Muker. The first section follows
the Pennine Way over the flanks of Kisdon to the west of the
Swale and is well waymarked. The return journey is southwards
along the opposite bank of the river and then westwards from
Muker.

ROUTE DESCRIPTION (Maps 15–17)

Start at the centre of the village facing the Kearton Guest House
and the shop *(1) (2)*. Turn R going down a side lane as far as a R-
bend; there, go through a stile in the wall to the L by a PW sign.
Turn R between a wall and a barn and go through two further
stiles. Immediately after the last stile turn L and cross a field to a
gap and then to a small bridge. On the opposite bank turn R and
follow a path by the stream; at the wall ahead the path bends L
and climbs up the hillside by the wall to a stile at the top. After
the stile turn R and follow the clear path which slowly climbs up
the hillside. (As you climb, glorious views begin to open up over
the dale to the R.)

At the top, meet a wall and follow it to a barn, here the path
goes half L to a stile (PW signs). Follow the wall on the L round
to a gate; beyond the gate follow the wall on the R as it bends R
and along to a farmhouse *(3)*. Go through the gate at the far end
of the house and then L through a second gate into a lane
between walls (PW sign). At the end, bend R with the wall and
then after 45 yards (40 m) turn back half L at a PW sign. Go up
the hill to a gap at a wall corner. Continue with a wall on the R.
The path now goes ahead across the hillside with wonderful
views down to the R into Swaledale. A succession of walls are
crossed at stiles, gates or gaps, but the path is clear and yellow
waymarks will be found throughout. After $1\frac{1}{2}$ miles (2.5 km)

90

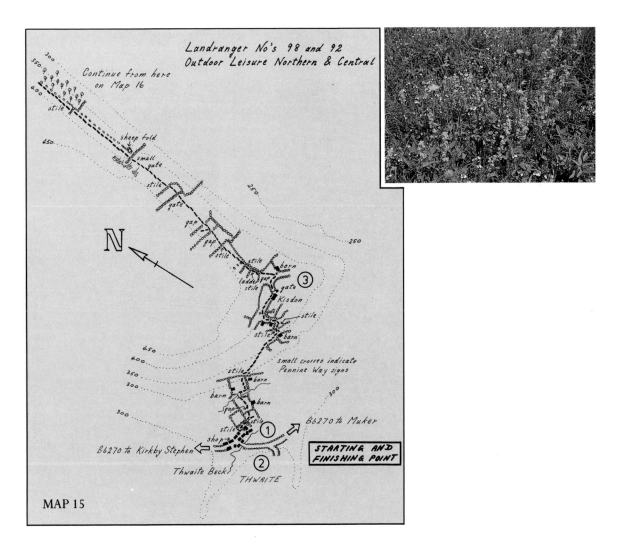

Landranger No's 98 and 92
Outdoor Leisure Northern & Central

Continue from here
on Map 16

sheep fold

small gate

stile

gate

gap

gap

stile

stile *barn*

③

ladder stile *gate*

Kisdon

stile

stile *barn*

*small crosses indicate
Pennine Way signs*

stile

barn

barn *barn*

gap

stile

stile

shop

① B6270 to Muker

B6270 to Kirkby Stephen ←

Thwaite Beck

②

THWAITE

**STARTING AND
FINISHING POINT**

N

MAP 15

(PW sign), towards the end of a long wood on your R, go R through a stile (PW sign) and descend to the R of a small scar. Meet a path lower down and turn L along it, soon to enter Keld (toilets and shop, but no pub) by the church.

Leave by the same path. After 250 yards (230 m) turn down L to a footbridge *(4)*. Cross and go up the path to the L to meet a farm road, there turn R along it soon crossing a bridge. Follow the farm road beyond for 2½ miles (4 km) keeping on or near to the R-bank of the Swale to a footbridge crossing it to the R. Cross and on the opposite side turn R to a stile and then on 45 yards (40 m) to a second stile. Follow the path which now goes half L across seven fields to the small village of Muker. At the village go through a gate and across a yard for a short distance to reach a road. Turn R and walk along the road between houses, at the end turning R to a stile and a gate by a house. (The church *(5)* to the L is well worth a short detour.)

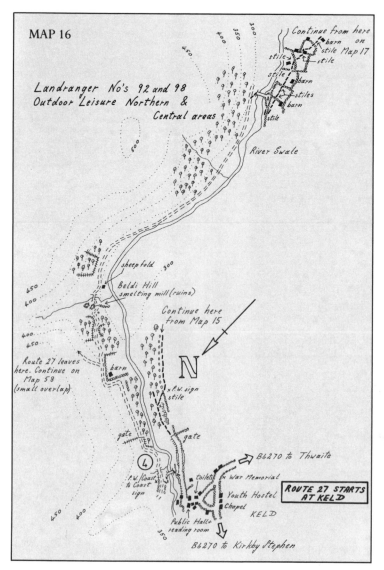

MAP 16

Landranger No's 92 and 98
Outdoor Leisure Northern &
Central areas

River Swale

Continue from here
barn on
stile Map 17
stile ... stile
stile
barn
stiles
barn
stile

sheep fold
Beldi Hill
smelting mill (ruins)

Continue here
from Map 15

N

Route 27 leaves
here. Continue on
Map 58
(small overlap)

barn

P.W. sign
stile

gate
gate

P.W./coast
to Coast
sign

toilets
War Memorial

B6270 to Thwaite

ROUTE 27 STARTS
AT KELD

Youth Hostel
Chapel   KELD

Public Hall &
reading room

B6270 to Kirkby Stephen

Go along a paved footpath with a wall on the L. This
continues across six fields. In the seventh field the path bends to
the L past a large barn to a stile to the R of a further barn; after
the stile turn L down a drive to the road. In the road turn R and
walk along to a bridge. Do not cross, but instead go through a
stile on the R and along the R-bank between the stream and a
wall. Cross a stile and then continue on this path over three
fields; at the end turn L over a small bridge and immediately R to
a stile. The path gradually leaves the stream to the L over three
small fields to reach a further stream. Continue on the R-bank of

Thwaite

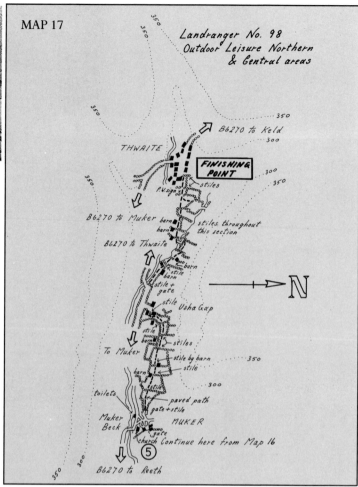

MAP 17

Landranger No. 98
Outdoor Leisure Northern
& Central areas

B6270 to Keld

THWAITE

FINISHING POINT

stiles

F.V. sign

B6270 to Muker   barn

barn   stiles throughout
                this section
B6270 to Thwaite

barn
stile
barn
stile +
gate

stile   Usha Gap

N

stile
barn   stiles
To Muker
stile by barn
barn   stile
stile

toilets
paved path
gate + stile

Muker
Beck   MUKER

gate
church   Continue here from Map 16
⑤

B6270 to Reeth

this stream to a stile and then follow a footpath back to
Thwaite.

1 Upper Swaledale

To many walkers Upper Swaledale has a special quality, that
is not to be found elsewhere in the Yorkshire Dales. Undoubtedly this is partly explained by its more remote situation in
the north of the Park, to which high and wild moorlands,
crossed by narrow and unfenced roads of impressive steep-
ness, impose a barrier. Partly, it must also be due to the
character of its villages: Keld, Muker, Thwaite and Gunnerside; small compact huddles of cottages — stone-walled and
flag-roofed — their position carefully chosen to give them
some protection against the rigours of the northern winter.
'Timeless' is always the word that comes to mind when you
visit them, at their best perhaps on warm summer evenings
when grey-blue smoke drifts from old chimneys and swallows

The Swale

and martins circle overhead; the music of running water providing a constant background, for each village rests on a stream, either on the Swale itself or on one of its tributaries.

In the eighteenth and nineteenth centuries Swaledale was one of the centres of lead mining, and the mouths of abandoned levels, hushes, spoil heaps and the ruins of old smelt mills are a common feature in most of the northern gills; occasionally, it must be admitted, disfiguring, but seldom less than fascinating. And, finally, the special character of Upper Swaledale lies partly in its place-names which are Scandinavian in origin; for Norsemen came into this area from the west early in the tenth century and, finding it much to their liking, settled there. Thwaite denotes a forest clearing, Muker a narrow field, Keld a spring, whilst Gunnerside was Gunnar's saetr or Gunnar's spring pasture. Common names such as beck, fell, gill and moss are also Old Norse.

2 *Thwaite*

Thwaite is perhaps best known to most as a watering place on the long trek up the Pennine Way. It was also the birthplace of the Kearton brothers, early pioneers of nature photography. On the wall of the schoolhouse in Muker, where they received their early education, two plaques were placed by public subscription: the first 'In memory of Cherry Kearton. Naturalist, author and explorer. Pioneer of wild life photography. July, 1871–Sept. 1940.' and the second '. . . in memory of Richard Kearton, FZS. Naturalist, author and lecturer. Born 2nd Jan. 1862, died 8th Feb. 1928.'

3 *The Corpse Way*

In the vicinity of Kisdon the line of an old road is crossed which ran from Keld to Grinton through Muker and Gunnerside. The oldest road in Swaledale, it became known as the Corpse Way, because it was the way along which corpses were carried from the upper dale villages to the nearest consecrated ground at Grinton. In extreme cases this involved a journey of about 15 miles (24 km), the corpses being carried in wicker coffins. Muker church was consecrated in 1580 as a Chapel-of-ease to Grinton, considerably reducing the journey, although the first people were not buried there until some years later.

4 *Kisdon Force*

As is the case with Wensleydale to the south, the base of Swaledale was formed in rocks of the Yoredale Series, although in this case at a higher level. The immediate result of this is a superb series of waterfalls formed over the bands of limestone both on the Swale itself and on its tributaries. Kisdon Force is passed on this route, Catrake and Wain Wath Force are a short distance north of Keld, and a further waterfall in East Grain is passed on Route 27.

5 *Muker Church*

Originally built in 1580 as a Chapel-of-ease to Grinton (see above) for the benefit of folk in the upper part of the dale, it was considerably extended in 1761, 1793 and again in 1890. The clock was placed in the tower to commemorate the coronation of George V and Queen Mary on 22 June, 1911.

THE ASCENT OF WHERNSIDE

STARTING AND FINISHING
POINT
Ribblehead (98-765793) at the
junction of B6255 and B6479
between Ingleton and Hawes
LENGTH
7½ miles (12 km)
ASCENT
1500 feet (460 m)

As the highest mountain in Yorkshire, Whernside inevitably attracts the crowds, although, in my opinion, both Ingleborough and Pen-y-ghent are superior. The old route up the mountain left from directly between Ivescar and Winterscales. This was always long and tedious, and with the passage of time it had also grown muddy — very muddy. An example of the damage that can be caused by thousands of heavy boots — and many not nearly so heavy — tramping up and down, day in and day out, throughout the year. For that reason, and in order to allow the ghastly scar on the face to grass over, an alternative route (which is in any case immeasurably superior and will therefore give a lot more pleasure) has been arranged by the National Park Authority. It is the route described here — a 'must' for railway enthusiasts.

ROUTE DESCRIPTION (Maps 18–20)

From the T-junction walk towards the railway bridge, turning R along the farm road just before the Station Inn. Continue past the viaduct *(1)* to a wall at the far end. Follow a path to the R of the railway to the Blea Moor signal box. After the box continue along the clear path to the R of the railway (and later with a stream) to an aqueduct over the railway line. Cross the aqueduct and follow the path beyond on the R side of the stream.

The large waterfall further along is Force Gill. From the vicinity of the Gill take a path which goes away to the R to the R of a fence. Follow this, later crossing the fence at a stile. Follow a path on the opposite side which curves half R across the moor. This later curves to the L and rises up to the summit ridge of Whernside. Turn L to the summit (OS obelisk).

Continue beyond the summit with the wall to your R. After about ¾ mile (1.2 km) descend over two small patches of scree; at the bottom of the second patch by a large cairn go half L and descend steeply to a ladder stile. Continue descending to a

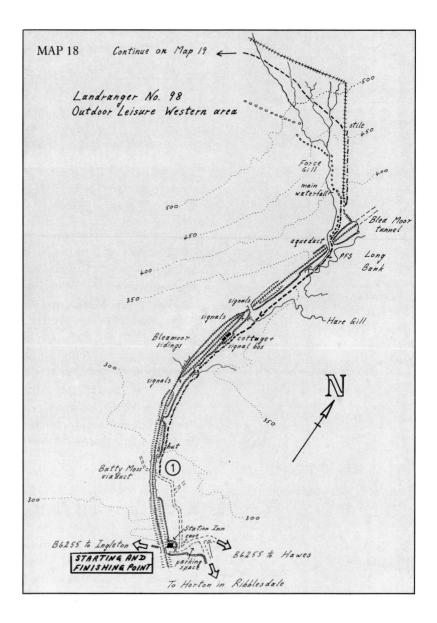

second ladder stile and then across a field to a third ladder stile in the far R-hand corner. Immediately after the stile go L through a small gate (i.e. to the R of a barn).

Head towards a farmhouse, passing through a gate and then to the R of barns to a small gate. Continue in the same general direction over four fields (there is a scar and a waterfall to the L) to Ivescar. Go between barns and the house, turning R before the final large barn. Turn L through a gate immediately after the barn and cross the field half R to a gate on the far side. In the next field follow the L-hand wall (crossing a fence) to a stile in the wall corner. Cross the next field to the R to a further stile and then across the final field keeping by the wall to a farm road. Turn

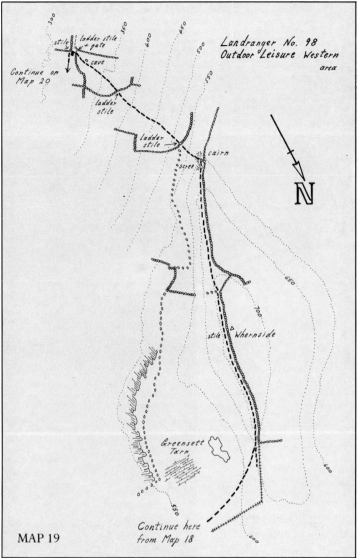

Landranger No. 98
Outdoor Leisure Western
area

Continue on
Map 20

stile
ladder stile
+ gate
cave
ladder
stile
ladder
stile
cairn
scree

N

stile Whernside

Greensett
Tarn

Continue here
from Map 18

MAP 19

L. After a gate across the road, turn R over a bridge and follow
the farm road back to Ribblehead.

1 The Settle–Carlisle railway

The construction of the Settle–Carlisle railway by the
Midland Railway Company, in the six years between 1869
and 1875, was a major achievement in civil engineering. The
aim of the project was to give the Midlands a main trunk
route from London to Scotland via Bedford and Derby,
which would enable it to compete with its main rivals, the
Great Northern Railway which operated the East Coast
Route through York and the London and North Western
Railway operating a West Coast Route through Crewe.

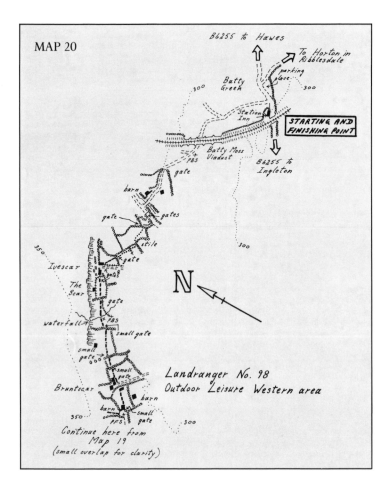

MAP 20

B6255 to Hawes

To Horton in Ribblesdale

parking place

Batty Green

Station Inn

STARTING AND FINISHING POINT

Batty Moss Viaduct

FBS

gate

B6255 to Ingleton

barn

gates

gate

gates

stile

gate

Ivescar

gates

The Scar

gate

waterfall

FBS

N

small gate

small gate

small gate

Bruntscar

barn

barn

small gate

Landranger No. 98
Outdoor Leisure Western area

FFS

Continue here from Map 19
(small overlap for clarity)

From the outset it was clear that the forcing of a line through an area of high fell and deep valleys would be a formidable one. Railway lines have to be relatively level, with a rise or fall of only a few feet in a mile, and fairly straight. It was these requirements which necessitated the profusion of viaducts, cuttings, embankments and tunnels which are characteristic of the Settle–Carlisle.

In the 72 miles (116 km) of track between Settle and Carlisle there are no less than twelve tunnels and fifteen viaducts. The Ribblehead Viaduct (originally Batty Moss Viaduct and so called on the Outdoor Leisure Map) has twenty-four arches, is a quarter of a mile long (400 m) and rises about 100 feet (30 m) above the ground; there are also six others with lengths of about 200 yards (180 m). The longest tunnel, the Blea Moor, is 2,629 yards (2.4 km) long with a depth of about 500 feet (150 m) at its deepest point.

Whernside from Greensett Tarn

The Ribblehead Viaduct

The construction of the line required a vast army of workers who were brought in from all over the country and housed in shanty towns along the line of work. Maiming and death from disease or accident were unfortunate, but common, features of everyday life. In the south porch of the Parish Church at Settle and on the west wall of the small church at Chapel le Dale are memorial tablets to those who lost their lives.

The two most impressive features of the line can be seen from Route 15, the Ribblehead Viaduct and the entrance to the Blea Moor Tunnel. On the moor slope behind the tunnel entrance are the shafts used in construction, and since for ventilation, with adjacent spoil heaps of excavated material.

CRUMMACK DALE AND THE NORBER ERRATICS

STARTING AND FINISHING POINT
Clapham National Park Centre car-park (98-746692)
LENGTH
8 miles (13 km)
ASCENT
1200 feet (370 m)

A superb walk, much of it along the lovely green lanes for which the Dales are famous, but the main features of interest are the Norber Erratics and the limestone pavements at the head of Crummack Dale.

ROUTE DESCRIPTION (Maps 21, 22)

Walk from the car-park into the road and turn R. Follow the road to the church. Just before the church, where the road swings L, turn R and then L by some gates to enter a lane (Thwaite Lane). Follow this lane uphill passing through short tunnels. At a lane junction at the top of the hill keep R (i.e. continue in the same direction), soon passing a wood. Immediately at the end of the second field on the L after the junction (i.e. approximately $\frac{1}{2}$ mile, 800 m, from the junction) turn L over a ladder stile (PFS 'Norber'). Go half R along a path towards a prominent scar. Near to the scar the path bends round a wall corner on the R to a further ladder stile. (Note here the large boulders from the crag above, which were used in the construction of the wall. The old dalesmen were never anxious to make unnecessary work.) Keep near to the wall until it bends away to the R, then keep in the same direction to a PFS. Make a short detour here by turning L up a small ravine to the open hillside above the scar, the Norber Erratics, i.e. large boulders *(1)* will now be seen over to the R.

Return to the PFS and go L (i.e. continuing in the original direction) across the hillside to reach a wall at a ladder stile. Beyond, go half L to a wall gap and then along a ledge under a scar to meet a wall. Follow the wall down to a lane. Cross the ladder stile opposite and turn L. Go over a stile in a fence and then a ladder stile at a wall. Continue in the same direction (no path) over pasture land, crossing three further stiles to reach a stream by two magnificent clapper bridges. Cross the R-hand bridge and then re-cross over the L-hand bridge (i.e. return to

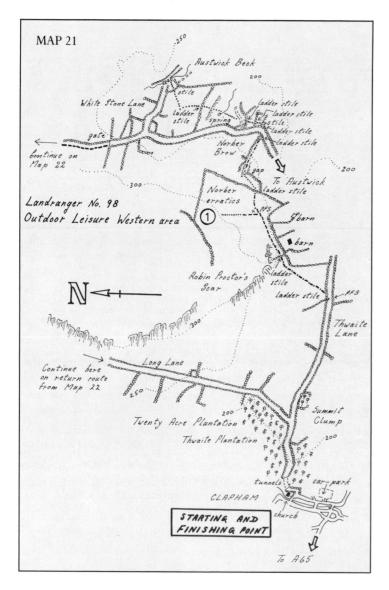

MAP 21

Austwick Beck

White Stone Lane

stile

ladder stile

ladder stile

ladder stile

spring

ladder stile

gate

Norber Brow

continue on Map 22

gap

To Austwick

ladder stile

Landranger No. 98
Outdoor Leisure Western area

Norber erratics

①

PFS

barn

barn

N ←

Robin Proctor's Scar

ladder stile

ladder stile

PFS

Thwaite Lane

Continue here on return route from Map 22

Long Lane

Twenty Acre Plantation

Thwaite Plantation

Summit Clump

tunnels

car park

CLAPHAM

STARTING AND FINISHING POINT

church

To A65

the same side) to the end of a lane (White Stone Lane). Go along the lane to a T-junction, turn R and follow the farm road to the farm of Crummack. Pass the farm keeping the wall on your R. Beyond the farm after a ladder stile take the grassy path which rises slightly L away from the wall. Follow this into the head of Crummack Dale.

After about $\frac{1}{2}$ mile (800 m), at a path junction, fork R along a path which rises to a ladder stile in a short length of wall crossing a break in the scar (Beggar's Stile). Immediately afterwards at a large cairn take a grassy path half L across an

Limestone scenery, Crummack Dale

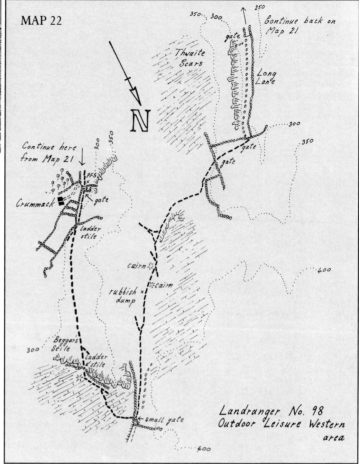

MAP 22

extensive area of limestone pavement. (It might be expected that this will give slow and difficult walking, but in fact the footpath is grassy underfoot and the very opposite will be found; route-finding is also relatively easy with the aid of cairns.) Where the pavements end, cross a grassy valley and rise up the slope ahead to a small gate. Look back from this point for a magnificent view.

Turn L and follow a track by the wall. The path soon leaves the wall and becomes clearer as it crosses the moor. At a junction go R to pass a rubbish dump. Pass a cairn and 150 yards (140 m) after a second cairn at a further junction (there is a small scar and pavements to the R) fork R. Follow the clear path slowly descending to the end of a walled lane. Follow this lane for 1½ miles (2.5 km) to a T-junction. Turn R and follow back to Clapham.

1 The Norber Erratics

The large boulders covering the hillside above Nappa Scars on

the western side of Crummack Dale are the famous Norber Erratics. Angular in shape and composed of dark grey Silurian gritstone they are obviously alien to the hillside for the predominant rock there is white limestone, clearly seen both lower down at Nappa Scars and in the extensive pavement area some 300 feet (90 m) higher. They originated at a lower level and about $\frac{1}{2}$ mile (800 m) away in Crummack Dale where the Silurian rock bed reaches the surface, and were transported to their present position by a glacier during the last Ice Age, to be left there when the ice finally retreated. The limestone bed, on which they were deposited, has been considerably dissolved away since that time so that some of the boulders now stand on short pedestals of rock, the height of which indicates the amount of solution that has taken place since the boulders were deposited (about 5 cm every 1000 years). Boulders such as these, which have been moved by glaciers and then left behind when they retreated, are called erratics.

Norber Erratics. The dark grey of the gritstone boulder stands out in sharp contrast to the white limestone base rock.

2·17

A ROUND OF MALHAM MOOR

STARTING AND FINISHING
POINT
Malham National Park Centre
car-park (98-900627)
LENGTH
9½ miles (15 km)
ASCENT
850 feet (260 m)

A superb route, through magnificent limestone country, which must rank as one of the finest walks — if not the finest — in the Yorkshire Dales. Gordale Scar, Malham Tarn and the Tarn House, Water Sinks, the dry valley of Watlowes and the great precipice of Malham Cove are the main attractions, but the walk is magnificent throughout. Somewhat timid walkers should note that a short — but easy — rock climb must be negotiated if they are to continue the route beyond the ravine at Gordale Scar.

ROUTE DESCRIPTION (Maps 9, 23, 24, 1 — see also pages 64 and 28)

Follow Route 9 as far as the lower waterfall in Gordale Scar. Continue up the ravine by climbing the rock step to the L of the fall. Although hands have to be used in the climb, most people will in fact find little difficulty here for the rise is both short and unexposed, and good handholds and footholds abound. Above the fall go half L up a clear path to reach the top.

Continue to a stile in a wall (PFS). Beyond the wall follow the clear grassy path which goes down a shallow trough between small rock edges and stretches of pavement. After ¾ mile (1.2 km) reach a road. Turn R in the road, but after a few yards leave it to the R along a rough farm road. Continue along this with a wall to your R eventually to reach a cattle grid by a wood. Do not cross the grid, but instead turn L and follow a wall past a wood (to the R) to reach another farm road by a few trees. Turn R over a ladder stile (i.e. to enter the Malham Tarn Nature Reserve) and follow the farm road around Malham Tarn *(1)* as far as Malham Tarn House *(2)*.

Return from the house to the gate at the entrance to the Reserve. After the ladder stile, immediately leave the farm road half R to pass to the L of a small wood. Continue ahead on a grassy path to reach a road by a parking area *(3)*. Here turn R,

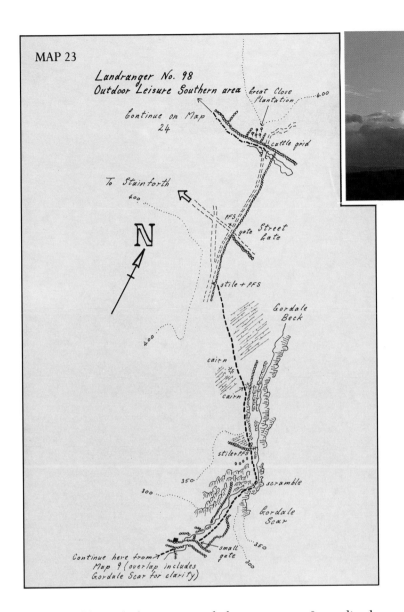

MAP 23

Landranger No. 98
Outdoor Leisure Southern area

Continue on Map
24

Great Close
Plantation

400

cattle grid

To Stainforth

400

N

PFS

gate Street
Gate

stile + PFS

Gordale
Beck

cairn

cairn

stile + PFS

350

300

scramble

Gordale
Scar

350

small
gate

300

Continue here from
Map 9 (overlap includes
Gordale Scar for clarity)

cross a ladder stile by a gate and then a stream. Immediately after the stream leave the road to the L through a gate and follow a fence up a hill. (To find the well-known Water Sinks *(4)* make a short detour to the L as follows: after about 150 yards (140 m) from the gate take a path half L which soon reaches a wall. Here the outflow stream from Malham Tarn disappears into the ground. After viewing, retrace your steps back to the fence and recommence your climb.)

Near to the hilltop where the fence bends R continue ahead along a clear path over the moor. Just before the descent into a shallow valley (there is a small limestone scar to the R) branch L on a faint path which soon grows more distinct. Descend to a wall corner and continue with the wall to your R to a small gate.

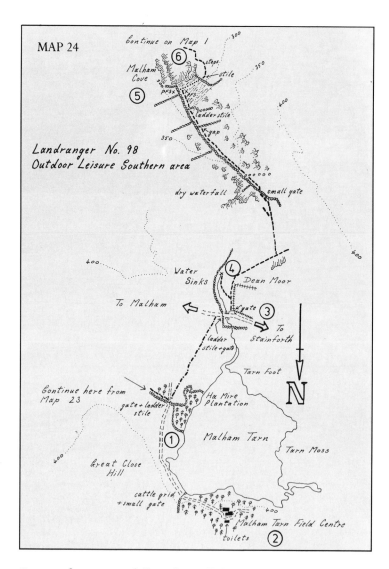

MAP 24

continue on Map 1

⑥

⑤

Malham Cove

PFS

ladder stile

gap

Landranger No. 98
Outdoor Leisure Southern area

dry waterfall

small gate

Water Sinks

④

Dean Moor

To Malham

gate

③

To Stainforth

ladder stile + gate

Tarn Foot

Continue here from Map 23

gate + ladder stile

Ha Mire Plantation

①

Malham Tarn

N

Great Close Hill

Tarn Moss

cattle grid + small gate

Malham Tarn Field Centre

toilets

②

Cross and turn L to follow the wall down into the dry valley of
Watlowes (note the dry waterfall to your L). The path follows
the wall through the valley to eventually reach a ladder stile
(*important note*: the edge of the Malham Cove precipice, which is
not fenced off, now lies approximately 150 yards (140 m)
directly ahead from the ladder stile. The precipice is sheer —
even overhanging — and very high. You have been warned!).

Continue ahead as far as a gate then a stile in the wall on the
L (PFS 'Malham Tarn'). Here turn R and cross the limestone
pavements *(5)* keeping well to the R of the cliff edge to reach a
stile on the far side. Cross and descend to the L down a steep
path. Lower down below the cliff turn L with the path heading
directly towards the stream. Near to the stream the path bends

The dry valley of Watlowes

to the R. (It is worthwhile making a short detour here to the L to the foot of the Cove where the stream emerges.) Follow the path keeping to the R of the stream eventually to reach a road *(6)*. Turn L and follow the road back to Malham. Or better still: go L over the stile from the road immediately after Beck Hall and follow a secluded footpath on the R bank of the stream back to the centre of the village.

1 Malham Tarn

A major fault line, the North Craven Fault, runs in an approximately east to west direction immediately to the south of Malham Tarn, so that the Great Scar Limestone on the north side is now considerably higher than that on the south. Little sign of this is now apparent on the ground, however, for the limestone face of the fault has been eroded back to its present position at Great Close, overlooking the Tarn; the process exposing the older and non-porous Silurian rocks beneath. It is on these that Malham Tarn was formed. Originally it was twice its present size for the low-lying areas to the east and west of the Tarn, Ha Mire and Tarn Moss, were also flooded. The present depth — at most 14 feet (4 m) — is maintained by an embankment and sluice gate to the south built by a previous owner, Thomas Lister, in 1791.

The Tarn, with its lime-rich water at a height of 1229 feet (375 m), is a highly unusual feature of great interest to naturalists. Appropriately enough it is now owned by the National Trust and managed as a nature reserve by the Field Studies Council.

2 Malham Tarn House

The fine house reached at the furthest point to Route 17 is Malham Tarn House, given (along with the Tarn and an adjacent farm) to the National Trust in 1946 by Mrs Hutton Croft. With the purchase or donation of three other local farms between 1964 and 1976 the total holding of the Trust in this area was raised to 3406 acres (1378 hectares). The House, Tarn and some adjoining land have been let to the Field Studies Council since 1947, the House being used as a Field Centre and the Tarn area as a Nature Reserve. Courses are held there between February and November inclusive.

There have been buildings on the site of the Tarn House for several hundred years, but the present House dates at the most from the eighteenth century. The main part of the house facing the Tarn was built by a Lord Ribblesdale who used it as a shooting lodge. The eastern wing and stables to the rear which form the courtyard were constructed by a later owner, Walter Morrison — wealthy industrialist and

Malham

Liberal Unionist Member of Parliament for Skipton Division — who lived there until his death in 1921.

Many famous people have visited Tarn House in its time. Of these, Charles Kingsley, who was there on several occasions and set his famous work *The Water Babies* in the surrounding countryside, John Ruskin, who left his influence upon the design of the House, and Charles Darwin, are perhaps the best known.

3 *The Pennine Way*

This was the first Long Distance Route created by the National Parks Commission (later the Countryside Commission). 250 miles (403 km) of glorious walking — most of it over high and lonely moors — from Edale in Derbyshire to Kirk Yetholm over the Scottish border. A large proportion (53 miles, 85 km) of the Way lies within the Yorkshire Dales National Park. It was appropriate, therefore, that Water Sinks Gate on Malham Moor was chosen for the official opening ceremony, held on 24 April, 1965, when the Way was opened at a gathering of 2000 ramblers by the then Minister of Land and Natural Resources, Fred Willey.

Although many people played a part in the creation of the Way there is general agreement the contribution of one man was outstanding. The name of Tom Stephenson, secretary of the Ramblers' Association from 1948 until 1968, will be for ever associated with it.

4 *Water Sinks*

Disappearing streams are a common feature of limestone country; the best-known example occurring just to the south of the Malham–Langcliffe road, where the outflow from Malham Tarn disappears quietly but decisively into the ground, at a spot known appropriately as 'Water Sinks'. It will be obvious however, to all who follow Route 17, that this was not always the case, for the shallow valley beyond, the 'dry waterfall' at Comb Scar and the further valley of Watlowes, leading directly to the lip of Malham Cove, were formed by water action, and mark the old course of the stream which must have produced at Malham Cove a spectacular waterfall nearly 250 feet (76 m) high. Occasionally, in very wet conditions, the stream will still flow further, but a flow over the Cove itself has not been observed since the beginning of the nineteenth century.

It must not be thought however that the stream now emerging from the base of the Cove is that which disappears underground 500 feet (150 m) higher at Water Sinks. Investigations towards the end of last century and more recently in 1972–73 by D. I. Smith and T. C. Atkinson, using water pulses, produced by opening the sluice gates feeding the stream at Malham Tarn, and by the injection of dyes at local sinks, have shown conclusively that this is not the case.

The Cove stream comes instead from Smelt Mill Sink, about $\frac{3}{4}$ mile (1.25 km) to the east, while that from Water Sinks emerges south of Malham at Airhead Springs, the two watercourses crossing each other underground at different levels.

Only under very exceptional conditions, paradoxically in times of drought or heavy flood, does any water find its way from Water Sinks to the Cove.

5 *Malham Cove* See page 30.

6 *Iron-age field boundaries* See page 32.

2·18

CARLTON MOOR

STARTING AND FINISHING
POINT
Carlton (99-064847). There is no car-
park in Carlton, but a few cars can be
left there with care.
LENGTH
9½ miles (15 km)
ASCENT
1450 feet (440 m)

A fine moorland walk, in one of the quieter areas of the Park, which crosses and re-crosses Carlton Moor between Coverdale and the valley of Walden Beck. The outward journey is to the south of the moor by the lonely farm of Fleensop and the return further to the north by Howdon Lodge. The best part is undoubtedly the descent from Fleensop Moor along an exceptionally fine moorland path of short springy turf. The views over the two dales from the higher ground, as would be expected, are excellent. The section around Fleensop has been extensively waymarked with yellow paint.

ROUTE DESCRIPTION (Maps 25–28)

From the chapel turn R and walk up the road *(1)*. Where the road bends L go up a minor road half R. Go L at a fork and continue to the end of the metalled road, here go through the gate ahead and along a farm road. Follow the farm road past a farm; then where it swings L go through a gate ahead and continue alongside a wall. Cross a further wall at a gap and immediately after a stream go L through a gate and continue in the same direction, but now on the opposite side of the wall. Where the wall ends go half L to a gate in a wall. Drop down to cross a stream and then pass through a gate on the far side. Follow the faint path beyond to the L of the stream eventually to reach a gate in a wall, then further along take the ladder stile over a wall (there is a coniferous wood to the L). Continue in the same direction to cross a farm road and a stream to reach a wall where turn R; go L through a gate just before a fence starts. Go to the R around the edge of the next field passing through a gate at a PFS 'To Barn'. Cross the field to the R of a large barn and then L behind it to a gate. Go ahead along the farm road between coniferous woods towards the farm of Fleensop.

Do not enter the farm but instead go over the bridge to the L and back along the opposite side of the small valley. After the wood on the R go R through a gate. Climb half L up the field to the top of a belt of trees where cross a stile, continuing with a

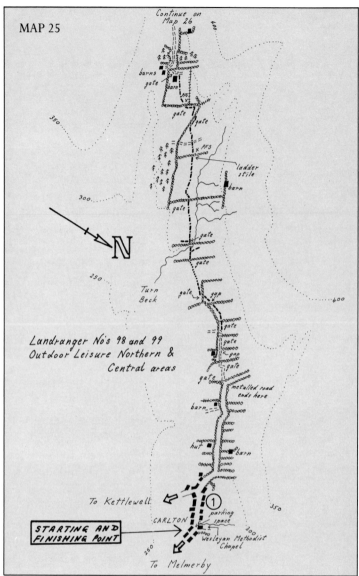

wall on the L to the moor top. At the top turn R and walk along the ridge following a wall. Later the path leaves the wall half R and crosses the moor to a gate in a wall. Cross into the rough moorland road beyond and turn R. Follow this for $1\frac{3}{4}$ miles (3 km) to the road in the valley of Walden Beck. This is undoubtedly one of the finest moorland tracks to be found anywhere, with splendid views ahead during the descent.

Turn R in the road and walk along it for 1 mile (1.6 km) to where a rough lane enters on the R (note an old chimney in the wall on the R). Turn R into the lane and follow it uphill, later bending R with it. Where the wall on the R ends take a track to the L; this runs up the R-hand side of the deep valley

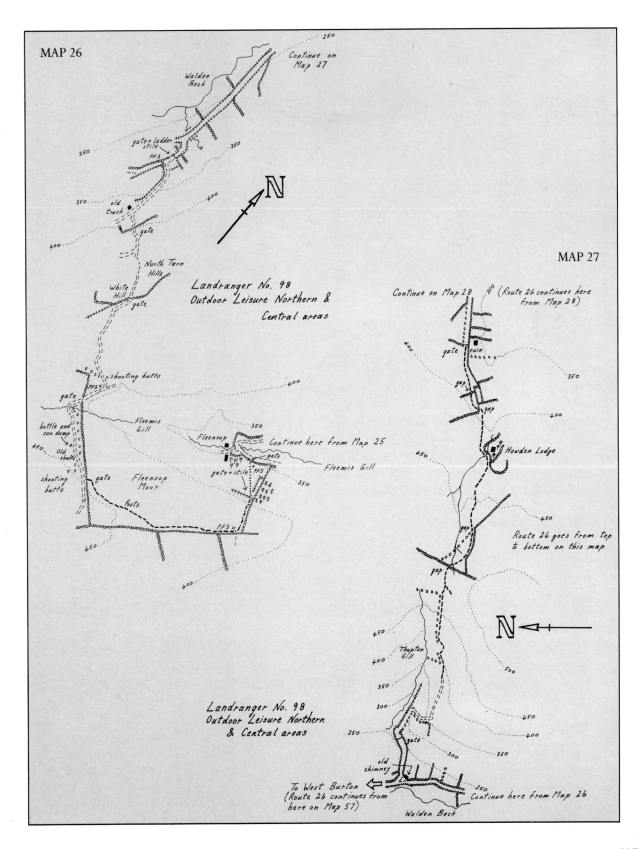

MAP 26

Walden Beck

Continue on Map 27

250

250

gate + ladder stile

PFS

350

350

old truck

gate

400

400

North Tarn Hills

White Hill

gate

N

Landranger No. 98
Outdoor Leisure Northern &
Central areas

shooting butts

PFS x l

gate

400

bottle and can dump

Fleemis Gill

Fleensop

350

Continue here from Map 25

450

Old shafts

gate

Fleensop Moor

gate + stile

PFS

Fleemis Gill

shooting butts

gate

350

Posts

450

PFS x l

400

MAP 27

Continue on Map 28

350

(Route 26 continues here from Map 28)

400

gate

ruin

350

gat

gap

400

450

Howden Lodge

450

gap

Route 26 goes from top
to bottom on this map

gap

N

450

Thupton Gill

400

500

350

300

450

250

gate

400

300

350

old chimney

To West Burton
(Route 26 continues from
here on Map 57)

250

Continue here from Map 26

Walden Beck

Landranger No. 98
Outdoor Leisure Northern
& Central areas

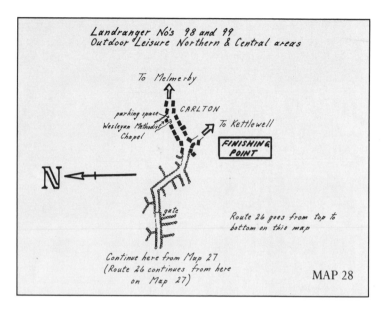

immediately visible ahead. Continue for about ½ mile (800 m) to the ridge top where a broken wall is crossed at a gap. Beyond the gap take the path half R to meet a further wall, here turn L descending with the wall to your R. Lower down at a ruined wall the path leaves the wall half L towards two groups of trees. At an old building by trees (Howden Lodge) bend L with the wall and then continue descending the moor leaving the wall on the R. At a wall corner go through a gap on the L and resume the same direction as before on the L of a wall. Reach the end of a green lane at a gate and follow it back to Carlton.

1 Henry Constantine

On the front of an old house in Carlton there is an inscription to Henry Constantine of Carlton who was known as the Coverdale Bard.

The inscription, dated 14 February, 1861, reads:

'He wrote from knowledge, genius kind
Opened the casket of his mind;
Poured out the essence to his worth
Endurance followed from his birth
Hope that blessed gift of Heaven;
Hope to every mortal given;
Hope which soothes the inward breast
Hope for Heaven's eternal rest'.

From Carlton Moor towards Wensleydale

GUNNERSIDE AND HARD LEVEL GILLS

STARTING AND FINISHING
POINT
Gunnerside in Swaledale
(98-950982). There is a small parking
space by the bridge.
LENGTH
10 miles (16 km)
ASCENT
1500 feet (460 m)

An extremely pleasant walk on excellent tracks over the moorland area to the north of Swaledale. By far the greatest interest, however, will be found in the numerous remains of the lead industry which once flourished in this area. There will be very few whose imagination will not be stirred by the old smelt mills, levels, hushes and spoil heaps which are passed along the way. The route follows Gunnerside Gill as far as the old Blakethwaite Smelt Mill, crosses Melbecks Moor to the east and then runs down Hard Level Gill to Surrender Bridge; footpaths high on the hillside above Swaledale lead back to Gunnerside.

ROUTE DESCRIPTION (Maps 29–31)

From the parking place cross the bridge and turn L by a café going upstream on the R-bank (PFS 'To Gunnerside Gill'). At the gate to Gunners Gill Hall turn R up some steps and go down a path between two walls, bending L at the end to resume the original direction. Follow the path to the R of the river crossing two walls. Eventually go through a small gate on the R and up some steps. The path turns back half R and then L at a PFS ('Gunnerside Gill/Gunnerside Village'). Follow the path parallel to the river crossing eight walls at stiles or gaps to reach some ruins *(1)*. (An alternative path is available on this section. For this, continue straight ahead from the steps, re-entering woodland; at the end of the wood continue over stiles to the ruin. The route has been waymarked.)

Beyond the ruin cross a stile at a fence corner and go up through a few trees to a wall. Keep on the path by the wall until you can cross it at a stile. Beyond follow a superb grassy path which climbs steadily up the hillside. Eventually reach some ruins. Pass these and continue parallel with the stream across the hillside to reach further ruins, Blakethwaite Mill *(2)*, at the junction of two streams.

Turn R up the hillside (no path) to reach a higher mine road.

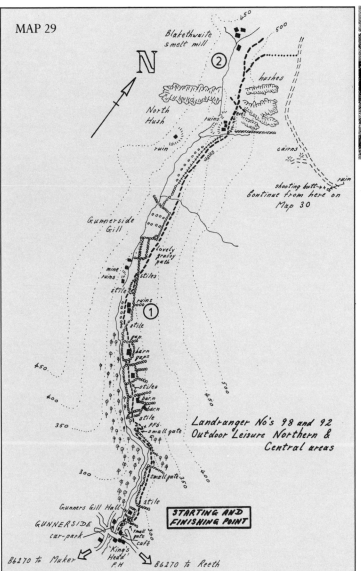

MAP 29

N

Blakethwaite
smelt mill

②

hushes

North
Hush

ruins

level

ruin

cairns

shooting butt
continue from here on
Map 30

Gunnerside
Gill

lovely
grassy
path

mine
ruins

stiles

stile

ruins

①

stile

gap

barn
gaps

stiles

barn

barn

stile

FFs.

small gate

small gate

Landranger No's 98 and 92
Outdoor Leisure Northern &
Central areas

stile

Gunners Gill Hall

GUNNERSIDE
car-park

small
gate
café

'King's
Head'
P.H

STARTING AND
FINISHING POINT

B6270 to Muker

B6270 to Reeth

Turn R along it and follow it across the moor top for $1\frac{3}{4}$ miles (2.8 km) passing numerous spoil heaps. Care should be taken here in mist or in snow as there are mine shafts in this area which may not be properly covered. Eventually the mine road descends into Hard Level Gill and crosses the stream over a bridge. Turn R on the far side and follow the mine road downstream for 2 miles (3.2 km) past the Old Gang Smelt Mill and Mine *(3)* to reach a road by a bridge. Surrender Smelt Mill *(4)* is only a short distance away at this point and well worth a visit; for this continue downstream along the path to the L of the stream. Afterwards return to the bridge.

Turn R (or L if coming from Surrender Mill) to cross the

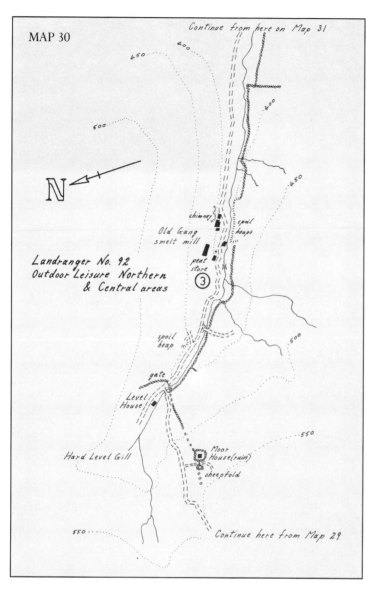

MAP 30

Continue from here on Map 31

450
400
500
400
450

N

chimney
spoil
heaps
Old Gang
smelt mill
peat
store
③

Landranger No. 92
Outdoor Leisure Northern
& Central areas

spoil
heap

500

gate

Level
House

550

Hard Level Gill

Moor
House (ruin)

sheepfold

550

Continue here from Map 29

bridge and climb up the hill on the road, going R at a junction after a few yards. At the top of the hill, opposite a shooting butt, leave the road half R over an earth bridge and follow a fairly clear and level path across the hillside. Eventually, reach a gate in a wall and follow the farm road beyond, soon bending L downhill. Pass several barns to reach a road, here turn R. Later the surface changes to two concrete strips; later still the road bends to the L. At this point, do not go with it, but instead continue in the same direction on a track. After $\frac{1}{2}$ mile (800 m) the path bends half R to a gate; immediately afterwards take a path half L descending to a wall. Continue to descend with the

Old Gang Smelt Mill

122

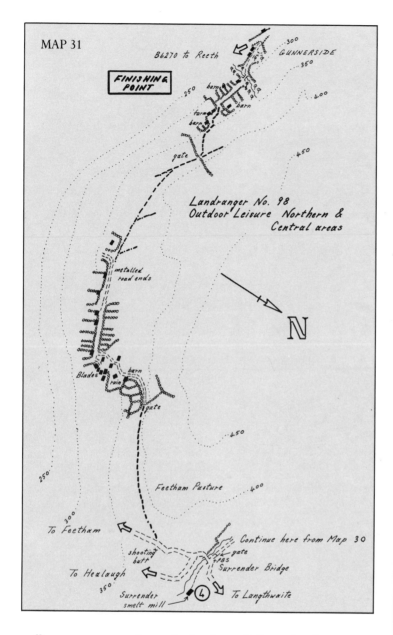

MAP 31

FINISHING POINT

B6270 to Reeth
GUNNERSIDE

barn
barn
turn
barn

gate

Landranger No. 98
Outdoor Leisure Northern &
Central areas

metalled
road ends

N

Blades
barn
ruin
gate

Feetham Pasture

To Feetham

Continue here from Map 30
gate
shooting
butt
FBS
To Healaugh
Surrender Bridge

Surrender
smelt mill
④
To Langthwaite

wall on your L to the end of a lane. Follow this lane, soon
crossing a small bridge. After the bridge bend L and continue to
descend, later with a wall on the L, to reach a farm road by a
house. Go down it to a road and then along that back to the
bridge in Gunnerside.

1 Gunnerside Gill

The first ruins encountered on this walk are those to the right
of the path: these are the remains of an old crushing mill. On

Gunnerside Gill

the opposite side of the stream is the Sir Francis Level, and the obvious metal cylinder a short distance further along was an air receiver used for operating pneumatic rack and mine ventilating machines. About $\frac{3}{4}$ mile (1.2 km) further along still the path passes by the remains of Bunton Level where there are several ruined buildings with large spoilheaps on both sides of the stream. The hillsides here have been extensively savaged by a number of hushes — ravines produced by lead miners (see page 19)—of which the huge North Hush on the western side is the most impressive.

2 *Blakethwaite Smelt Mill* See page 175.

3 *Old Gang*

The extensive ruins passed on the way down Hard Level Gill are those of the Old Gang Mine and Smelt Mill. Mining was carried out around this site during the seventeenth century, but an extensive development of them took place during the eighteenth century. The first smelting mill on this site was built about 1770 by Lord Pomfret and his son-in-law (although there was a mill working in the previous century a short distance away); this was incorporated into a second mill constructed in 1805. The mill continued to work until about 1885. Coming down the Gill, there are a number of old levels on both sides of the stream. On the hillside to the left will be seen the pillars and end walls of the long peat store and further along the remains of the mill itself with its long flue rising up the hillside behind. The first mill was sited against the hillside where the flue rises, whilst the 1805 mill was nearer to the path. There are extensive spoil heaps across the stream.

4 *Surrender Smelt Mill*

The ruins, a short distance above Hard Level Gill from the bridge, are those of the Surrender Smelt Mill. The mill was built about 1839 on a site occupied by an earlier smelt mill, and continued in operation until about 1880. The building further along was a peat store and the line of the long horizontal flue can be easily distinguished across the moor.

Note: The remains of the old mines and smelt mills around Swaledale and elsewhere, however unsightly some may consider them, are a part of the history and of the heritage of this region. They deserve our respect. The passage of time will have its own effect upon them, it needs no help from those who find their pleasure in pulling down masonry or in daubing walls with names or trivial slogans. These remains have more than a touch of magic about them, each act of senseless damage reduces it by a little.

Simon's Seat and the Valley of Desolation

STARTING AND FINISHING POINT
Bolton Abbey car-park (104-071539)
LENGTH
11 miles (17.5 km)
ASCENT
1200 feet (370 m)

An extremely attractive and popular walk which combines some of the most beautiful parts of the Wharfe valley between Bolton Abbey and Howgill with the grand moorland of Simon's Seat. The moorland section is on Barden Fell which is covered by an Access Agreement (see page 186). An easy walk for category 3.

ROUTE DESCRIPTION (Maps 10, 32–34, 10 — see page 71)

Follow route 10 as far as the bridge to the Cavendish Pavilion. Do not cross, but continue on the R-bank of the river for $\frac{3}{8}$ mile (600 m) to reach a road. Turn R and follow the road up a hill to reach Waterfall Cottage (this will be on your L). Go through a small gate to the R of the cottage and follow a path across the field beyond to a small gate on the far side. Continue on a lovely grassy path which descends to a ford over a stream. On the far side of the stream turn R and go up on the L-hand bank past a waterfall and a bridge *(1)*.

Eventually, at a path junction, follow the main path half L up a hill to a stile. After the stile turn R in the forest road and follow this through the forest to a gate. Continue in the same direction on a clear moorland road for $1\frac{3}{4}$ miles (2.8 km) to the OS obelisk on Simon's Seat (there are two path junctions along the way, keep L at each) *(2)*.

For the descent from Simon's Seat go round to the L of the summit rocks to pick up a prominent path (PFS 'Daleshead only'). Descend the hillside. At a junction, follow the path to the R (sign). Cross a wall at a ladder stile by a gate and continue down a clear path through zig-zags to a gate in a lower wall. Cross into a lane and turn L.

Follow the lane through a farm for 1 mile (1.6 km) to a café and camp site (i.e. on your R). 150 yards (140 m) after the café turn R at cross tracks and follow the path to a road. Go down the lane opposite, bending R by a farm, to a river. At the river bank turn L. Follow the path along the L-hand bank for $1\frac{1}{4}$ miles

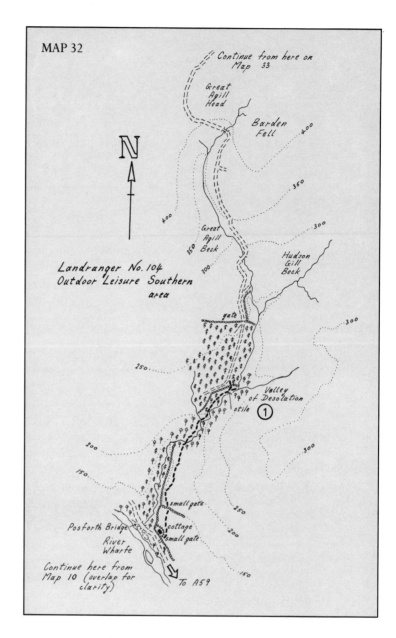

MAP 32

Continue from here on Map 33

Great Agill Head

Barden Fell

400

350

300

Great Agill Beck

Hudson Gill Beck

N

Landranger No. 104
Outdoor Leisure Southern area

400

250

300

gate

300

250

Valley of Desolation

stile ①

200

300

150

250

small gate

200

cottage
small gate

150

Posforth Bridge

River Wharfe

Continue here from Map 10 (overlap for clarity)

To A59

(2 km) to a road. Turn R along the road and immediately before Barden Bridge (3) go through a gate on the L. (From this bridge a short detour can be made to Barden Tower (4). Do not go through the gate, but instead cross the bridge and go up the road. At a junction turn L for a few yards. Afterwards return to the bridge.)

From the gate follow a path to the L of the river, crossing two stiles, to an aqueduct over the river. See Route 10 for the return route to the Bolton Abbey car-park from this aqueduct. Use the lower path through the woods to include the Strid (5) which was not visited on the outward journey.

Opposite *The Valley of Desolation*

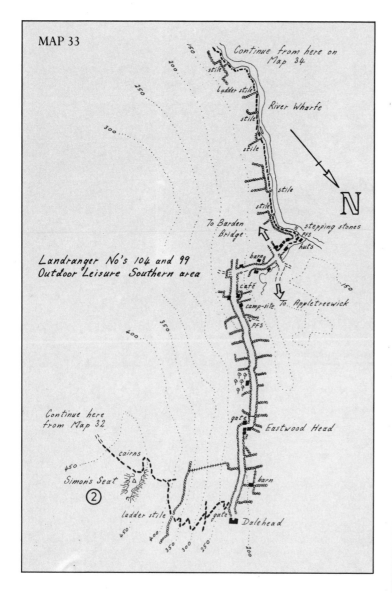

MAP 33

Continue from here on
Map 34

150

stile

200

ladder stile

250

River Wharfe

stile

300

stile

N

stile

stepping stones

To Barden
Bridge

PFS

huts

Landranger No's 104 and 99
Outdoor Leisure Southern area

barn

café

150

camp-site

To Appletreewick

PFS

350

400

Continue here
from Map 32

gate

Eastwood Head

cairns

450

Simon's Seat

barn

②

450

ladder stile

400

350

300

250

200

gate

Dalehead

1 The Valley of Desolation

The valley above the waterfall has been called the Valley of Desolation. It acquired this name after a severe storm in 1826 which caused considerable damage. Today, however, the · name is scarcely appropriate for the tree-cloaked slopes, attractive stream and the two waterfalls, one 50 feet (15 m) high, make it instead a place of sylvan beauty.

2 Simon's Seat

This name is given to the shapely outcrop of millstone grit at the top of the fell. As with most other gritstone outcrops

Simon's Seat

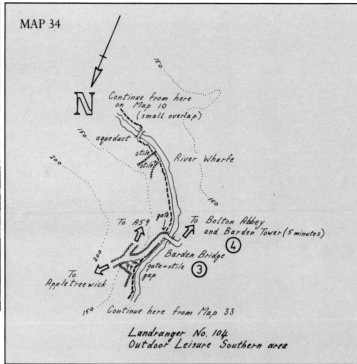

rock-climbing is practised at Simon's Seat with routes up to about 70 feet (20 m).

3 *Barden Bridge*
The very narrow but elegant bridge of three spans which crosses the Wharfe is Barden Bridge. An inscription cut into the parapet tells us that 'This bridge was repaired at the charge of the whole West Riding, 1676'. Masons' marks can be seen on the stonework.

4 *Barden Tower* See page 160.

5 *The Strid* See page 72.

ARKENGARTHDALE

STARTING AND FINISHING POINT
Reeth (98-039993)
LENGTH
11½ miles (18 km)
ASCENT
1600 feet (490 m)

Arkengarthdale is the most northerly of the National Park dales, running from Reeth to the north-west between the summit of Calver Hill and the imposing line of Fremington Edge. This route runs in a clockwise direction around Calver Hill over Reeth Low Moor, crossing the Dale at Langthwaite, and returning along Fremington Edge. The moorland tracks of short springy turf over Reeth Low Moor are superb, as are the views later in the walk from Fremington Edge, but followers of the television series *All Creatures Great and Small* will be more impressed perhaps by the old bridge in Langthwaite which was featured in the programme.

ROUTE DESCRIPTION (Maps 35–37)

From the green at the centre of Reeth turn up Silver Street (B6270) by the Buck Hotel. Walk past the fire station and beyond the houses for 350 yards (320 m), then turn R up a narrow path between walls (PFS 'Skellgate'). Follow this delightful lane through L and R bends to its end at a gate. Continue ahead along a clear path with a wall to the L, contouring the hillside.

After ¾ mile (1.2 km) where the wall bends L, continue ahead to a junction where go L, dropping down by a house (Moorcock House) to a lower farm road. Turn R, soon passing a farm on your L. 200 yards (180 m) after the farm go R at a junction. Soon pass a wall on your L and shortly afterwards go R at a further junction for a few yards to another wall. Continue with this wall on your R. Where the wall bends round to the R, continue in the same direction (no path) soon picking up a path which climbs the ridge ahead. Continue over the ridge on the path which soon becomes much clearer. Follow the path across the moor to a gate by a road (the famous 'water-splash' featured in the television series *All Creatures Great and Small* is just down to the left).

Do not go through the gate, but turn back half R along a very obvious track. Follow this magnificent moorland track of short

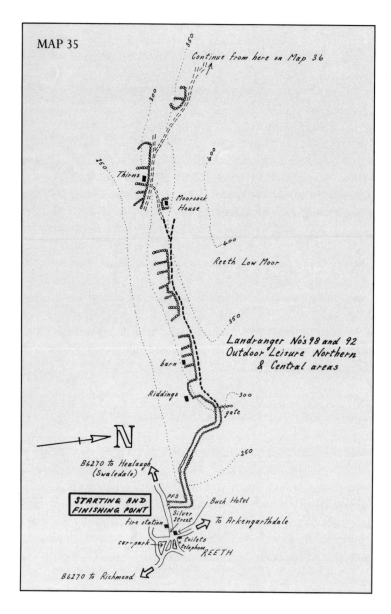

MAP 35

Continue from here on Map 36

Thirns

Moorcock House

Reeth Low Moor

Landranger No's 98 and 92
Outdoor Leisure Northern
& Central areas

barn

Riddings

gate

N

B6270 to Healaugh
(Swaledale)

STARTING AND
FINISHING POINT

PFS   Buck Hotel

Silver
Street   To Arkengarthdale
fire station

car-park   toilets
telephone   REETH

B6270 to Richmond

springy turf between massed banks of heather for $1\frac{1}{4}$ miles (2 km), gradually descending to the road in Arkengarthdale *(1)* — there is just one path junction on the way, at this keep L. Turn L along the road and follow it to the village of Langthwaite.

In the village turn R over the bridge and immediately R again on to the river side. Follow the path downstream on the L bank of the river. After $\frac{1}{2}$ mile (800 m) the path leaves the river to the L through a wood; at a PFS at the far end of the wood go L (i.e.

Reeth

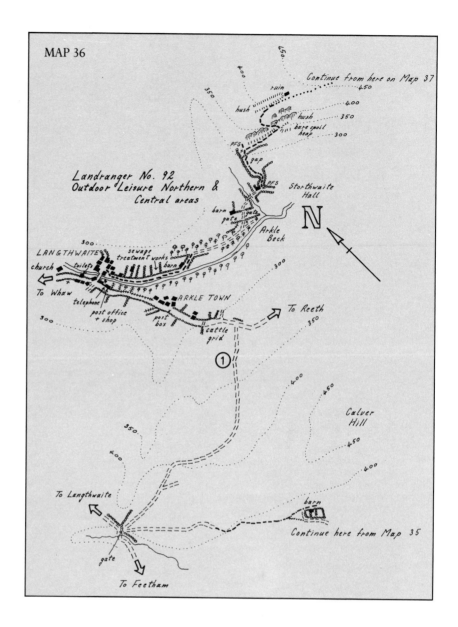

to Fremington). Follow the farm road to a footbridge by a ford, cross and go to the farmhouse ahead. Immediately after the first house turn L up a lane (PFS 'Hurst'). Where the lane ends continue up the field with a wall on your L to a wall gap at the top of the field. Turn R (PFS) and go up to the R of a hush (a ravine produced by lead miners — see page 19).

After 400 yards (370 km), at the foot of a large bare spoil heap, turn back half L climbing up a grassy path. The path soon bends R and goes to the R of a second hush. Where this hush ends, continue in the same direction over the moor by some spoil heaps (no path) to reach a gate at a wall corner. Go through the gate and continue in the same direction along

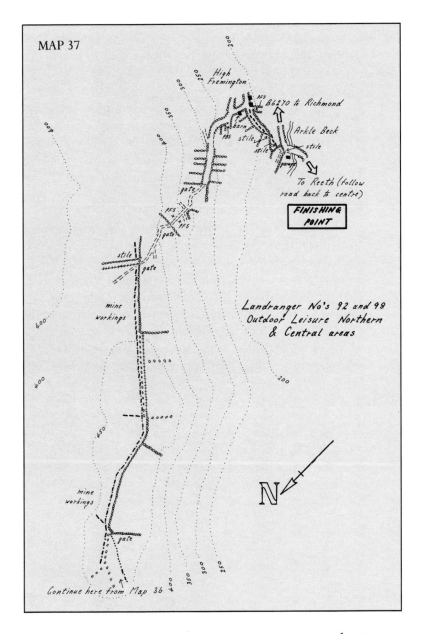

MAP 37

High
Fremington

PFS
B6270 to Richmond

Arkle Beck

barn
stile
PBS
stile

stile

garage

To Reeth (follow
road back to centre)

FINISHING
POINT

gate

PFS
PFS
gate

stile

gate

mine
workings

Landranger No's 92 and 98
Outdoor Leisure Northern
& Central areas

200

400

400

450

400

mine
workings

gate

N

Continue here from Map 36

300
250
350
400

Fremington Edge with a wall to your R. Continue for 1¼ miles (2 km) to a stile in a crossing fence.

Do not cross the stile, but instead go through a gate on the R. Descend the hillside on a clear path, later reaching a road. Lower down the road descends through a wood and immediately afterwards bends L with a bridleway (PBS 'Arkengarthdale') coming in on the R. Continue along the road for 55 yards (50 m) more then, where the road bends L, turn R down a narrow path. At the bottom turn R on the road and then almost immediately leave it again to the R at a gate and stile. The path beyond follows the wall soon passing through a stile. Further along cross

over another stile on the L and then over two meadows to reach
a road near to a bridge. Go R over the bridge back to Reeth.

1 Arkengarthdale

As with those of upper Swaledale the place-names of
Arkengarthdale show signs of Norse settlement. Arkengarthdale itself is 'the valley of Arnkell's (or Arkil's) enclosure',
Arnkell being a common Old Scandinavian name, whilst
Langthwaite was 'a long clearing'. At the mouth of the Dale
the influence is Anglian, however, as shown by the 'tun'
villages, such as Grinton and Fremington.

The Dale was an important centre for lead mining,
particularly from the beginning of the seventeenth century,
the miners living in local villages, such as Langthwaite, Whaw
and Arkle Town. Several hushes can be seen on both sides of
Slei Gill and there were smelt mills both there and further up
the Dale near Langthwaite. Considerable depopulation of the
Dale took place in the nineteenth century due to the decline
of the industry, with mining families moving southwards to
the Lancashire cotton towns and eastwards into Durham.

The Calf and the Eastern Howgills

STARTING AND FINISHING POINT
Sedbergh (97-657921)
LENGTH
11 miles (18 km)
ASCENT
2300 feet (700 m)

Although a part of the Yorkshire Dales National Park in the extreme north-western corner, the area of the Howgills is tied geologically, politically and socially to Cumbria rather than to North Yorkshire. It is a splendid region of great whale-backed hills — smooth, steep-sided and grassy (for there is little heather or bracken in the Howgills) — crossed only by lovely green tracks, with superb views both over the Dales and into the Lakes. Essentially, at present, an area for connoisseurs of walking, for the hordes who climb Ingleborough and Whernside, and think them marvellous, have yet to discover it. This is one of the best routes in the Howgills, up the long ridge past Winder and Arant Haw to the summit of The Calf and then down White Fell to Castley. Part of the Dales Way is followed back to Sedbergh.

In cloudy conditions proficiency with map and compass is essential in the Howgills.

Route Description (Maps 38-40)

From the church in Sedbergh take the Kirkby Lonsdale road (A683) past the post office, turning R after 50 yards (45 m) at a junction (sign 'Howgill 2¾'). Follow the road up a hill and past some playing fields; 85 yards (80 m) after a telephone box turn R up a lane (PFS 'To the Fell'). Soon reach a farm, go through a gate directly opposite and up a short lane which leads to a further path opening on to the open fell. Turn L and follow the boundary wall for about 200 yards (180 m) then, immediately after a small wood, turn half R up the hillside on a grassy track. Soon reach a crossing track and turn R along it. Follow this grassy track through bracken as it climbs slowly up the flanks of Winder. Eventually, at a cairn, the track swings L and goes up on the L side of Settlebeck Gill to the top of a ridge.

On the ridge meet a crossing track and turn R along it. Follow this very clear and grassy path as it slowly climbs, first on

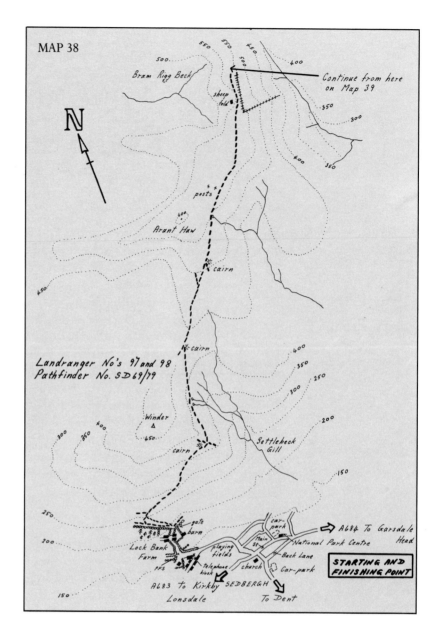

MAP 38

Bram Rigg Beck

sheep fold

Continue from here
on Map 39

posts

Arant Haw

cairn

cairn

Landranger No's 97 and 98
Pathfinder No. SD 69/79

Winder
△

cairn

Settlebeck
Gill

gate
barn
Lock Bank
Farm
PFS
telephone
kiosk
car-
park
Main St
National Park Centre
Back Lane
church
Car-park
A684 To Garsdale
Head

STARTING AND
FINISHING POINT

playing
fields

A683 To Kirkby
Lonsdale
SEDBERGH
To Dent

the ridge top and then over to the R; later the path dips into a
spectacular col and crosses it to a fence on the opposite side.
Climb to the L of the fence, turning sharply to the R with it
later. 200 yards (180 m) from the fence corner at a cairn on the
hilltop turn L and cross the open moor (no path) away from the
fence to pick up a clear path. Follow this path to the OS obelisk
at the summit of The Calf.

Continue beyond the obelisk in the same direction picking up
a path after a few yards; follow this to a crossing track and turn
L along it. This path goes alongside a ridge and then later
descends steeply on its L side. Eventually after a long descent

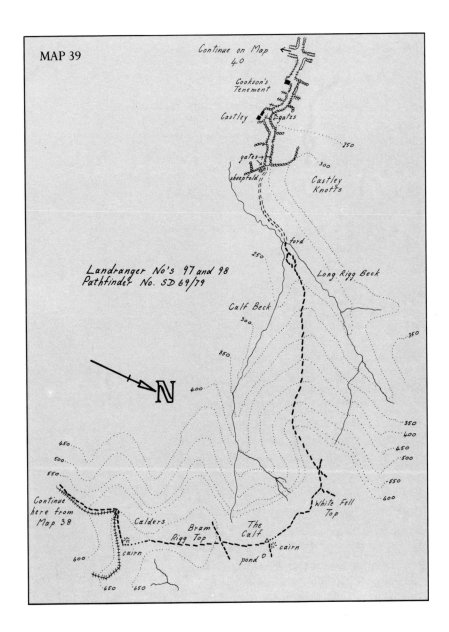

MAP 39

Continue on Map
40

Cookson's
Tenement

Castley ⬛ gates

gates→

sheepfold

Castley
Knotts

250

300

ford

Long Rigg Beck

250

Landranger No's 97 and 98
Pathfinder No. SD 69/79

Calf Beck

300

350

350

N

400

350
400

450
500

450
500

550

550

600

Continue
here from
Map 38

White Fell
Top

Calders

Bram
Rigg Top

The
Calf

cairn

600

cairn

pond

650   650

reach a stream junction. Cross the R-hand tributary at a ford and go downstream on a farm road. At a gate cross into a green lane and follow this, later metalled, for ⅔ mile (1.2 km) to a cross roads. Turn L.

Walk along the road for about ½ mile (0.8 km) to a bridge. Immediately after the bridge turn R through a gate and walk along a minor road past a small church, at a house continuing up the road half L. At the top the road bends L to reach two gates at a junction, turn R and follow a farm road down to a farm (Thwaite). Do not enter the farm, but instead turn L and then R between two farm buildings to a gate, here immediately turn L

141

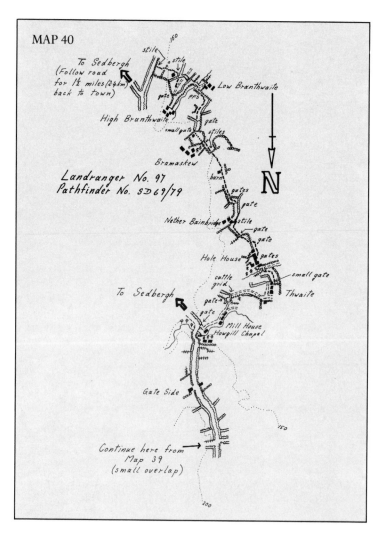

MAP 40

To Sedbergh
(Follow road
for 1½ miles (2.4km)
back to town)

stile   160   stile
Low Branthwaite
High Branthwaite   gate
small gate   stiles
Bramaskew
barn
Landranger No. 97
Pathfinder No. SD 69/79   gates
gate
Nether Bainbridge   stile   gate
gate
Hole House   gates
cattle
grid   small gate
To Sedbergh   Thwaite
gate
gate
Mill House
Howgill Chapel
Gate Side
150
Continue here from
Map 39
(small overlap)
200

through a small gate and go along the hillside to the R of a hedge. Where the hedge bends L drop down to a footbridge. Go L up the lane beyond, through a small gate and between a house and a barn into a farmyard (Hole House). At the end of the farmyard go between the last two barns on the R (two gates), then turn L and climb to the R of a hedge to a gate. Cross to the wall opposite and turn L, soon turning R through the first of two gates. Follow a wall to a farm (Nether Bainbridge), going through a stile to the R of a large barn and R again down the lane beyond.

At the end of the lane go through a gate and then half L through double gates, continuing to a small barn. At the barn go half L up a hill to a stile and then on to a further stile to the R of another farm (Bramaskew). Continue across the next field

The Lakeland fells in the distance seen from Arant Haw, Howgills

142

Sedbergh

beyond the farm to a gate to the R of a small hut, this leads into a lane which goes to the next farm of Low Branthwaite. Go through the gate to the L of this farm (PFS) and over a bridge into a lane, follow this to the last farm (High Branthwaite). Do not enter the farm, but turn back half R at a junction just before. Follow the farm road for a few yards beyond a gate then go half L across the field to a stile. Turn L after the stile up another field to reach a road at the top. Turn L in the road to a T-junction, and then R for $1\frac{1}{2}$ miles (2.4 km) back to Sedbergh.

3·23

BETWEEN LITTONDALE AND WHARFEDALE

STARTING AND FINISHING
POINT
Car-park at Buckden in Wharfedale
(98-943773)
LENGTH
11 miles (18 km)
ASCENT
2350 feet (720 m)

This walk follows the Dales Way along Wharfedale from Buckden to Starbotton, and then crosses Moor End Fell to Arncliffe in adjacent Littondale. The return journey to Buckden is over Old Cote Moor from Litton, a few miles higher up the dale than Arncliffe. As a high priority is given to inter-dale routes by the Park Authority, all the footpaths have been extensively way marked. Arncliffe is one of the most beautiful villages in the National Park, and Littondale and Wharfedale are two of the most beautiful Dales.

ROUTE DESCRIPTION (Maps 41-44)

Leave the car-park past the toilet block and cross over to the Hubberholme road opposite. Walk down the road and over the bridge. Immediately after the bridge turn L and go along a path on the R-bank of the river. After $\frac{1}{4}$ mile (400 m) at a PFS, just before the river bends L, turn half R to a small gate at a wall corner. Beyond, turn L along the hillside to a farm road and go to the L along it. Pass a barn and at a junction (PFS) go down L to a gate. Now continue ahead over a small footbridge to a gate and then along a path between walls; at the end go over another footbridge and through a small gate. Pass to the L of a barn and over a ladder stile ahead. Now continue along the path with a wall to your R to reach the river again at a ladder stile much further along. From there keep on the path to the R of the river as far as the bridge at Starbotton (PFS).

Do not cross the bridge, but instead turn R and follow a path which goes between broken walls, soon bending to the L behind a barn. The clear path rises slowly up the hillside, later passing through a wood. Leave the wood at a small gate and continue up the hillside to a ladder stile over a wall. After the stile, climb straight up the hillside to a gap in a wall; beyond, go half L for a short distance then continue straight up the moor towards a wall corner. Continue to climb with the wall first on the R and

145

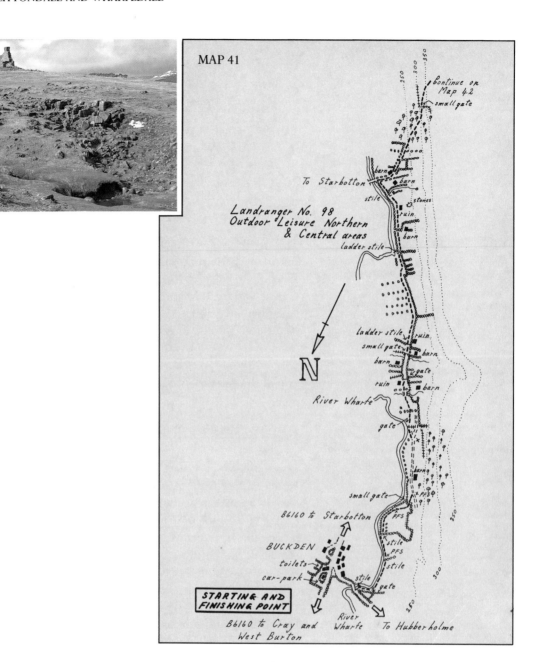

MAP 41

continue on
Map 42
small gate

To Starbotton

Landranger No. 98
Outdoor Leisure Northern
& Central areas

barn
barn
stile
stones
ruin

ladder stile

barn

ladder stile · ruin
small gate
barn
barn
gate
ruin · barn

River Wharfe

gate

N

barn

small gate

B6160 to Starbotton

PFS

BUCKDEN

toilets
car-park

stile
PFS
stile

STARTING AND
FINISHING POINT

stile
gate

B6160 to Cray and
West Burton

River
Wharfe

To Hubberholme

then on the L (crossing at a gap) until a ladder stile over a wall on the crest of the ridge is reached. On the far side start to descend along a path to eventually meet a farm road at a gate near a shooting hut. Continue down the farm road to a metalled road in the valley.

Turn L along the road, keeping R at a junction, to reach the bridge in Arncliffe. Immediately after the bridge turn R down a lane. At a road cross a bridge and go down a further lane opposite. At the end of the lane go over a ladder stile and cross the field beyond to a stile in the far L-hand corner. Go across the

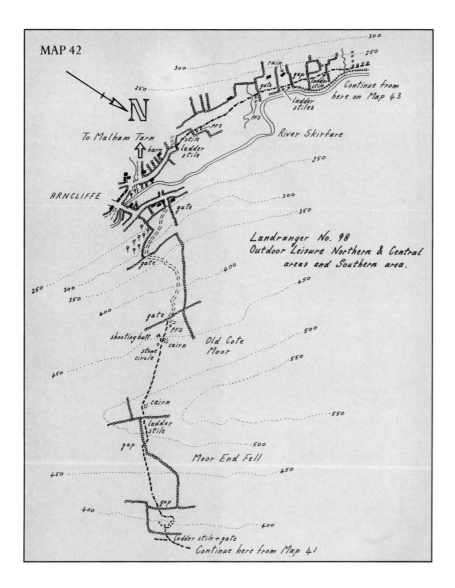

Continue from here on Map 43

very large field following to a gate in a wall (PFS) and then over two further fields to a ladder stile in a wall. Keep in the same direction with the river and fence to the R, crossing several walls, eventually passing a ruin to reach the river bank over a stile.

Immediately turn L through a small gate, then R to resume your original direction. After two further stiles reach the river bank again through a gate. Walk along the L bank between a wall and the river for 600 yards (550 m), then turn L through a gate (PFS). Cross the field beyond on a path to a wall corner (PFS) and then walk on to the L of a wall. Before reaching a farm go R through a gate (PFS) and cross to a further gate leading into a lane, there turn R to a bridge, then L to a road.

Go to the R along the road as far as *The Queens Arms* public

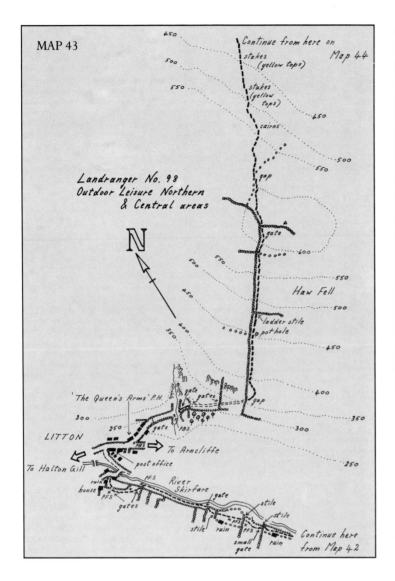

MAP 43

Continue from here on
stakes
(yellow tops)
Map 44

stakes
(yellow tops)

cairns

450

500

550

500

550

gap

Landranger No. 98
Outdoor Leisure Northern
& Central areas

N

600

450

550

500

Haw Fell

550

500

ladder stile
pot-hole

450

350

400

450

500

gate

400

The Queen's Arms' P.H.
gate
gates

300

250

gate
PBS

gap

400

350

300

LITTON

To Arncliffe

250

To Halton Gill

post office

PFS

PFS
ruin
house

River
Skirfare

gate

gates

stile

stile

gates

stile

ruin

PFS

ruin

small
gate

Continue here
from Map 42

house (passing a shop and tea house on the R). Turn L up the
lane in front of the public house; where the lane ends, cross a
stream, go through a gate just ahead and continue in the same
direction with a wall on the R. After the next gate take a track
which leaves the wall half L and goes up the hillside. Cross two
walls, the second at a gap. Immediately after this gap turn L and
start climbing straight up the hillside to the R of the wall just
crossed. After $\frac{3}{4}$ mile (1.2 km) reach a gate in a crossing wall at
the top of the ridge.

Beyond the gate, the path goes half L with the wall for about
100 yards (90 m) then leaves it to the R to cross a corner to a

Arncliffe from Brayshaw Scar

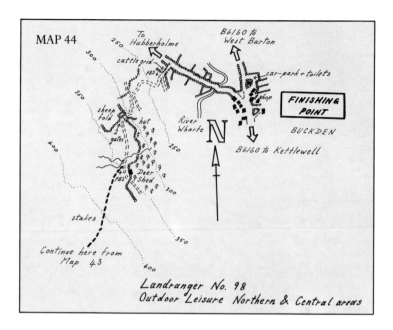

further wall. There turn R and continue down with the wall on
your L for 125 yards (115 m), then cross it through a gap. The
path now leaves the wall half L to descend the moor. The path is
clear and well-marked, first with cairns and then with stakes.
Eventually after 1 mile (1.6 km) reach a farm road above a
wood. Turn L and follow this farm road to a gate which leads
into sheep folds. In the folds go through a further gate directly
opposite and then down a farm road to a metalled road in the
valley. Turn R back to Buckden.

3·24

MASTILES LANE

STARTING AND FINISHING
POINT
Arncliffe (98-932718)
LENGTH
13½ miles (22 km)
ASCENT
1400 feet (430 m)

For centuries Mastiles Lane, running for 5 miles (8 km) across Malham Moor from Kilnsey to Street Gate, was part of a busy and important highway for the movement of pack-trains and drove herds; nowadays it is primarily a walking route and the predominant features of it are peace and solitude. Arncliffe, one of the most beautiful villages in the Dales, Malham Tarn and the imposing overhangs of Kilnsey Crag are some of the other highlights of this walk, but it is the superb walking over Malham Moor that will be best remembered.

ROUTE DESCRIPTION (Maps 45–49, 11 — see also page 76)

In Arncliffe *(1)* turn down the lane to the R of *The Falcon* public house (PFS 'Malham'). After a large house on the R a stream runs in the lane for a short distance; at its end turn R over a ladder stile (PFS) and rise half L to a ladder stile in a wall corner. Continue to follow the path which rises to a third ladder stile and then along the edge overlooking Cowside Beck; further along the path leaves the edge half L. No difficulty should now be found in following the path further as it crosses open ground for it is fairly clear, without any junctions and marked with cairns at helpful points. Several walls are crossed at ladder stiles which are also a great aid in route-finding. After about 2 miles (3.2 km) from the lane at Arncliffe reach the farm of Middle House. Pass the farm to the R and follow a wall as it bends to the L to reach a ladder stile. After the stile do not descend the hillside immediately ahead, but instead go half R across the moor to a ladder stile over a fence. Beyond, follow a faint path to the L of a fence; at the end where the fence bends R go ahead dropping down to the shore of Malham Tarn *(2)*.   Turn L and follow the rough drive along the shore of the tarn to a gate at the entrance to the nature reserve *(3)*. Continue on this drive beyond the gate for ½ mile (800 m) to reach a metalled road at a corner; here turn L for approximately 150 yards (140 m) to a gate. This gate is the start of Mastiles Lane *(4)*.

Follow the path beyond the gate with a wall on the R for 650

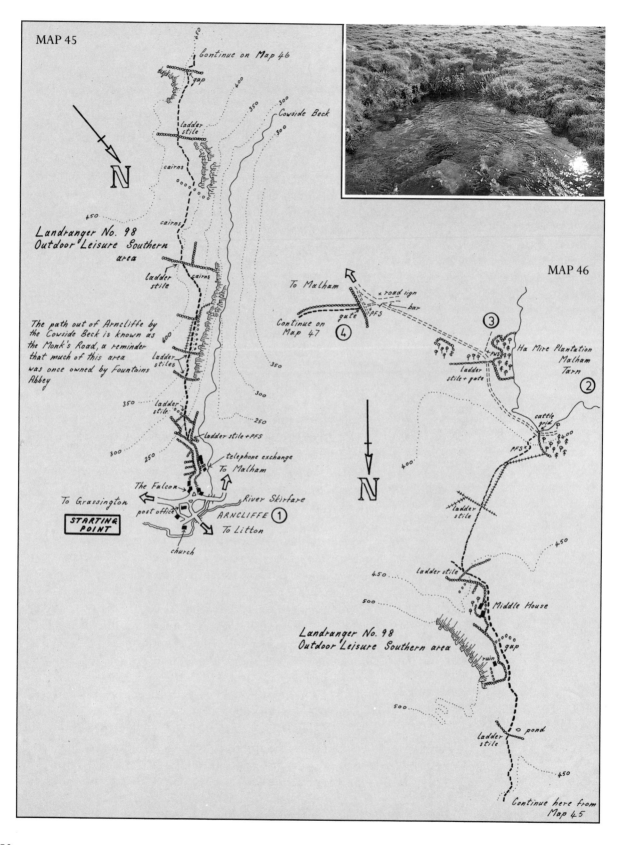

MAP 45

Continue on Map 46

gap

Cowside Beck

ladder
stile

cairns

Landranger No. 98
Outdoor Leisure Southern
area

cairns

ladder
stile

cairns

The path out of Arncliffe by
the Cowside Beck is known as
the Monk's Road, a reminder
that much of this area
was once owned by Fountains
Abbey

ladder
stiles

ladder
stile

ladder stile+PFS

telephone exchange
To Malham

The Falcon

To Grassington   River Skirfare

post office

STARTING
POINT   ARNCLIFFE ①

To Litton

church

MAP 46

To Malham   x road sign   bar

Continue on   gate   PFS
Map 47 ④

ladder
stile+gate

Ha Mire Plantation
Malham
Tarn

②

cattle
grid

PFS

ladder
stile

ladder stile

450

500   Middle House

gap

ruin

500

ladder   pond
stile

450

Landranger No. 98
Outdoor Leisure Southern area

Continue here from
Map 45

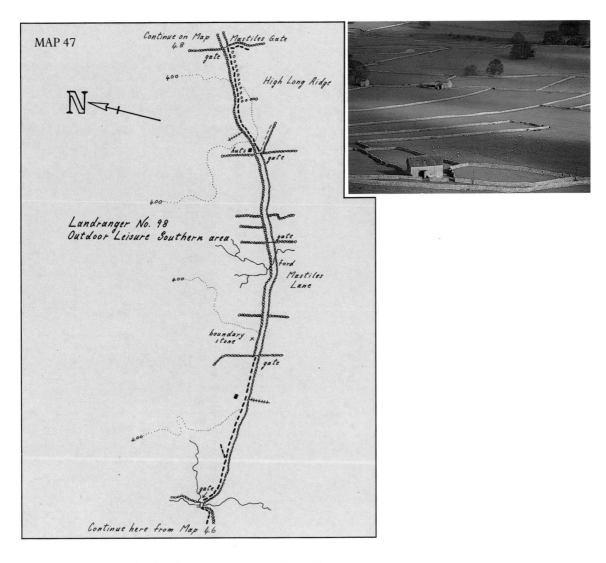

yards (600 m) to a footbridge. Cross and go through the gate ahead to continue in the same direction with a wall still on the R. Eventually reach the end of a walled lane and go along this for 1 mile (1.6 km) to its end at a gate. Immediately after the gate take the path to the L at a fork and follow this with a wall on the L to where the walled lane resumes. Continue along the lane between walls for a further $1\frac{1}{2}$ miles (2.4 km) to its end, then keep in the same direction along a rough road to reach a metalled road. Turn R and descend to the main road (B6160) at Kilnsey (5).

Turn L and walk along the road for $\frac{3}{4}$ mile (1.2 km) to a road junction; here go L (i.e. on the road to Arncliffe). Reach Sleets Gill Bridge by a small wood after a further $\frac{3}{4}$ mile (1.2 km). After the bridge watch for the first wall coming in on the R and go through a gate immediately afterwards. Go half R to a gap in a

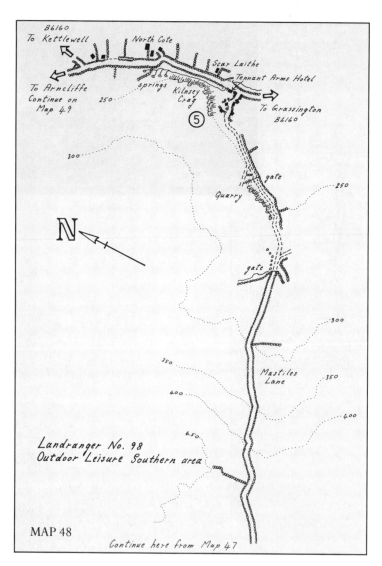

fence and a small ruin, and then half L along the hillside through two wall gaps towards a cottage. Pass to the L of the cottage and round a wall corner to a gate. Continue along the farm road beyond, passing a ruined barn, to reach a road by the bridge at Hawkswick.

See Route 11 (page 75) for the return to Arncliffe.

1 Arncliffe

This is one of the prettiest villages in the Yorkshire Dales, with a large village green surrounded by stone-walled and flag-roofed old houses. Its name was recorded in the Doomsday Book of 1086 as Arneclif and is Old English for 'eagles' cliff'. The present church was built in 1450, probably

Mastiles Lane. The descent towards Kilnsey

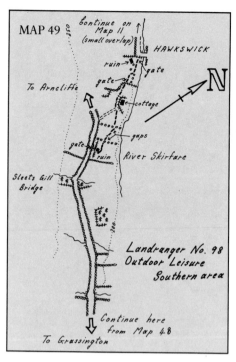

on the site of a Norman church of the twelfth century. Extensive rebuilding was carried out in 1793 and 1840, however, so that the tower is the only part of the original church which now remains.

2 *Malham Tarn* See page 112.

3 *The Pennine Way* See page 113.

4 *Mastiles Lane*

The early history of Mastiles Lane, as with many other ancient tracks, is obscure, although its original name of Strete Gate is suggestive for the word 'straet' was commonly used in Saxon times, possibly, but not certainly, in relation to a road. From the twelfth up to the late eighteenth or early nineteenth centuries, however, the lane served as an important highway for the movement of stock and goods. From about 1150 to the Dissolution this would be in large part monastic traffic, for the lane was part of an administrative link between Fountains Abbey near Ripon, one of the most important abbeys in Britain, and its extensive holdings on Malham Moor and beyond; flocks of sheep, herds of cattle, packhorse trains and monastery employees would be common sights along the lane. These activities continued after the Dissolution for the area remained important for wool production and also served as a valuable link for the movement of drove herds to and from the markets held on Malham Moor. Only with the development of canals and railways did the traffic die away.

The walling around and along Mastiles Lane was a product of the Enclosure Movement in the late eighteenth and early nineteenth centuries.

5 *Kilnsey Crag*

The huge overhanging cliff of Great Scar Limestone to the left of the road is Kilnsey Crag; it was formed in the Ice Age by a glacier which ground its way down Wharfedale. It is one of the most important climbing cliffs in the Yorkshire Dales, the first major route there, the Original Route, being completed in 1957 by Ron Moseley. Today there are over thirty routes, a number of which give over 200 feet (60 m) of climbing. Kilnsey is one of the few climbing crags near to a main road and a line of parked cars is a sure indication that climbers are at work there. Climbing may only be undertaken with the consent of the landowner.

3·25

A ROUND OF BARDEN MOOR

STARTING AND FINISHING
POINT
Strid car-park (104-059563) on
B6160 2½ miles (4 km) north of
Bolton Abbey.
LENGTH
13 miles (21 km)
ASCENT
1600 feet (490 m)

The area of Barden Moor, about 4 miles (6.5 km) north-east of Skipton, is covered by an Access Agreement made with the Trustees of the Chatsworth Settlement in 1968 (see page 186). It is an area of wild moorland; wet, rough and covered with thick heather and bracken, with weird outcrops of weathered millstone grit along its edges, in marked contrast to the limestone uplands only a few miles away. Few paths cross this area and once off them the walker will find the going slow and arduous. This route follows some of the best features of the moor: the reservoir road to Upper Barden Reservoir, the western edge with its outcrops and spectacular views and the waymarked bridleway from near Rylstone Cross. A section to Thorpe Fell Top and beyond to the western edge is over rough and open moor and best followed on compass bearing.

ROUTE DESCRIPTION (Maps 50–53)

Leave the car-park by the road entrance and turn R. Follow the road to just past Scale Farm where a road comes in from the L, turn L along it. (Barden Tower is only 400 yards, 365 m further along the road at this point and is well worth a short detour *(1)*.) Immediately after the forest turn R through a gate (i.e. opposite the minor road). Walk along this superb but rough moorland road for about 2¾ miles (4.5 km) passing Lower Barden Reservoir — taking the R-fork at the junction just before to pass it on its R-hand side — and up to the house at the north-east end of the dam of Upper Barden Reservoir *(2)*.

Immediately before the Reservoir Keeper's house turn back half R along a track (PFS 'Burnsall'). Later at a junction keep L on the main track and follow it to a small dam on Gill Beck, approximately 1 mile (1.6 km) from the house. Continue for a few yards to a path junction and bear L. Follow this path to the R of Gill Beck to a shooting cabin (note the old chimney to the L

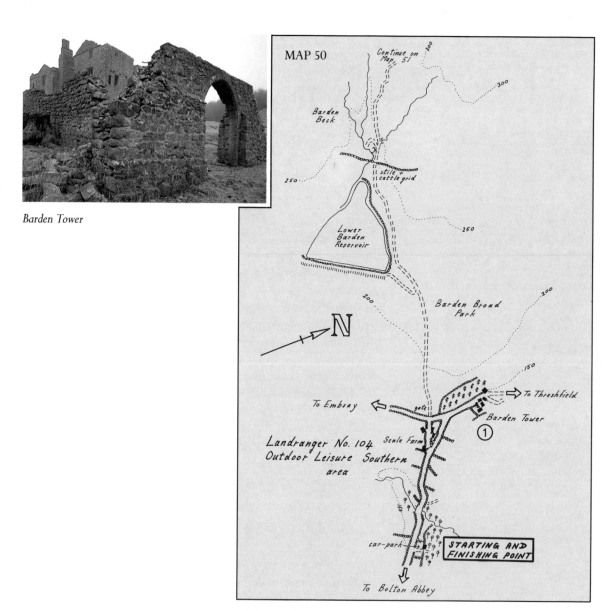

Barden Tower

of the track). From there cross the moor on a bearing of 254°
magnetic to reach — if your compass work is accurate — the
triangulation pillar on Thorpe Fell Top. Leave the Top almost
due east (bearing 285° magnetic) over open moor to reach a wall
after ½ mile (800 m).

Turn L and follow the wall along the edge of the moor. The
views to the west over Cracoe and Rylstone are spectacular.
Continue past the obelisk on Watt Crag and the cross on
Rylstone Fell, keeping by the wall. From the cross continue to
follow the wall, descending to reach a bridleway which crosses
the wall at a gap about 600 yards (550 m) from the cross. This
bridleway is marked by blue paint waymarks at the gap and
short blue-topped posts on each side.

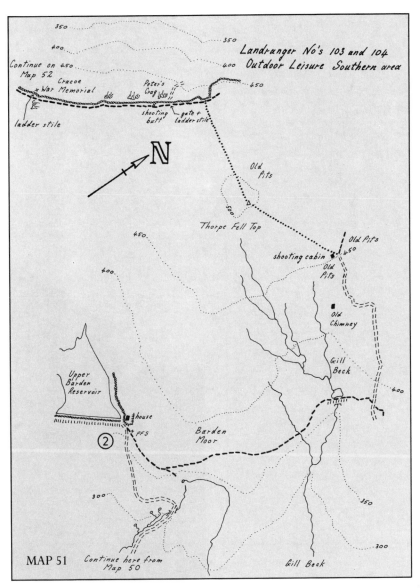

Turn L and follow the bridleway away from the wall and over the open moor. The path is — at the time of writing — indistinct, the way long, the moor itself singularly featureless. No difficulty should be found, however, for wooden posts (with blue tops) have been placed at short regular intervals across the moor so that, even in mist, the next one will be located before doubt can take too firm a hold. After $\frac{3}{4}$ mile (1.2 km) pass to the L of shooting huts and later at a junction (PFS/PBS), just past some shooting butts, keep R. The path gradually improves to form an excellent walking surface. Keep on this moorland track to eventually reach a road. Turn L over a cattle grid and follow the road back to the T-junction passed earlier in the day; there turn R and return to the car-park.

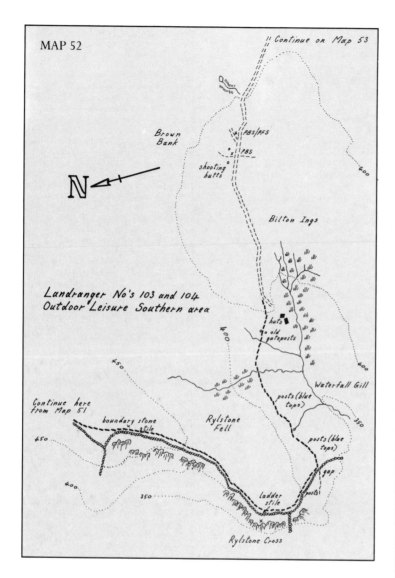

MAP 52

Continue on Map 53

Brown Bank

PBS/PFS

PBS

shooting butts

Bilton Ings

Landranger No's 103 and 104
Outdoor Leisure Southern area

huts

old gateposts

Continue here from Map 51

boundary stone

stile

Rylstone Fell

Waterfall Gill

posts (blue tops)

posts (blue tops)

gap

posts

ladder stile

Rylstone Cross

1 Barden Tower

Barden Tower was originally one of six lodges built for forest keepers in about the eleventh century. It became the property of the Clifford family in 1310, although none lived there regularly until Henry Clifford, the tenth Lord, came in 1485. During his time there the Tower was considerably extended and a chapel added to the neighbouring Priest's House. Following his death in 1523 the Tower was used as an occasional dwelling and hunting lodge but had fallen into ruin by the end of the century. In 1643 Lady Anne Clifford inherited the estates and, after ordering considerable resto-

Rylstone Cross on a misty day

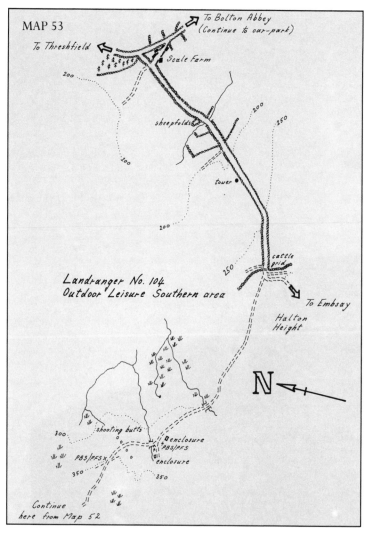

MAP 53

ration, lived there from about 1659 until her death in 1676. A plaque at Barden Tower records her work there.

The Tower became the property of the Dukes of Devonshire in 1748 and is now in the care of the Trustees of the Chatsworth Settlement. It has not been lived in since Lady Clifford's death and has been in ruins since c.1800.

2 The Barden Reservoirs

The moors covered by the Access Agreement are the gathering grounds for two reservoirs — Lower and Upper Barden. These were constructed in 1874 and 1882 respectively by dams across Barden Beck to supply water to Bradford. Due to the rapid growth in that city during the late nineteenth century, these soon proved insufficient and further reservoirs were constructed in Nidderdale above Pateley Bridge — the Gouthwaite (1901), Scar House (1936) and Angram Reservoirs (1919) — just outside the National Park boundary.

Wensleydale and Coverdale

STARTING AND FINISHING
POINT
Aysgarth Falls National Park Centre
car-park (98-012888). Travelling
from Hawes along the A684 turn L
about ½ mile (800 m) after Aysgarth,
the car-park is on the left soon after
crossing the bridge.
LENGTH
14 miles (23 km)
ASCENT
1750 feet (530 m)

Starting at Aysgarth Falls the route follows the Ure on its south side as far as West Witton, then south to Melmerby and Carlton in Coverdale. A splendid moorland track leads back over Carlton Moor to West Burton and Aysgarth. The walk along the Ure is the finest in Wensleydale and West Burton is widely regarded as the prettiest village in the Dales. The views from Carlton Moor over Coverdale and the valley of Walden Beck are superb.

ROUTE DESCRIPTION (Maps 54–56, 28, 27, 57 — see also pages 118 and 117)

Leave the car-park into the road and turn R. Immediately after the bridge *(1)* go up some steps directly ahead and to the R of the Carriage Museum, these lead into the churchyard. Go through the churchyard turning to the L behind the church *(2)* to a stile. Cross the field beyond to a second stile which leads into a small wood. On leaving the wood, go half L across a field to a wall overlooking the river, there turn R and continue parallel to the river going through several stiles and passing the Lower Falls. In the last field before a farm (Hestholm) go half R (PFS) to the far R-hand corner. Go into the road and turn L.

Immediately after a bridge and bends in the road, go L through a stile (i.e. before the AA box on R). Pass to the L of a barn and, in the next but one field, continue to the R of a farmhouse crossing a ladder stile by a gate. Cross two further fields and in the third field reach the river bank once more. Continue by the river; later the path goes up to the R through a small wood to a ladder stile (PFS). Cross the field beyond half L to a stile on the top of a steep bank, immediately after crossing go L through a second stile and continue in the same direction as before, with a fence to the R, to a ladder stile. Keep by the wall as you continue in the same direction across three fields to reach a wood. Cross the wall over a ladder stile near to the corner and take a path half L through the wood to reach the

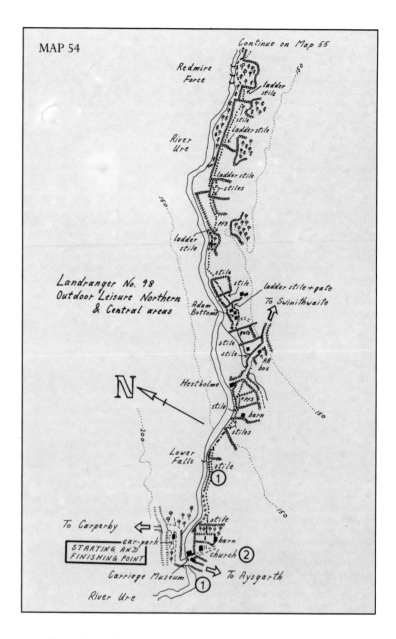

river bank by Redmire Force. Above the falls, the path goes half
R away from the river to cross a wall by a corner. Continue in
the same direction with a wall and the river to the L. Eventually,
cross a small stream and follow a path to the R (i.e. leaving the
river) as it zig-zags and then heads across a field. At a path fork
go R, curving round to meet a wall on the R and on to the end of
an overgrown lane. Follow this lane to the road at West Witton.

Turn R in the road then L at a junction. Follow the road up
the hill going L at a T-junction and then R at a fork by Penhill
Farm. Continue climbing on the road until you reach the top of
the hill. Go over the top and descend on the unfenced road on

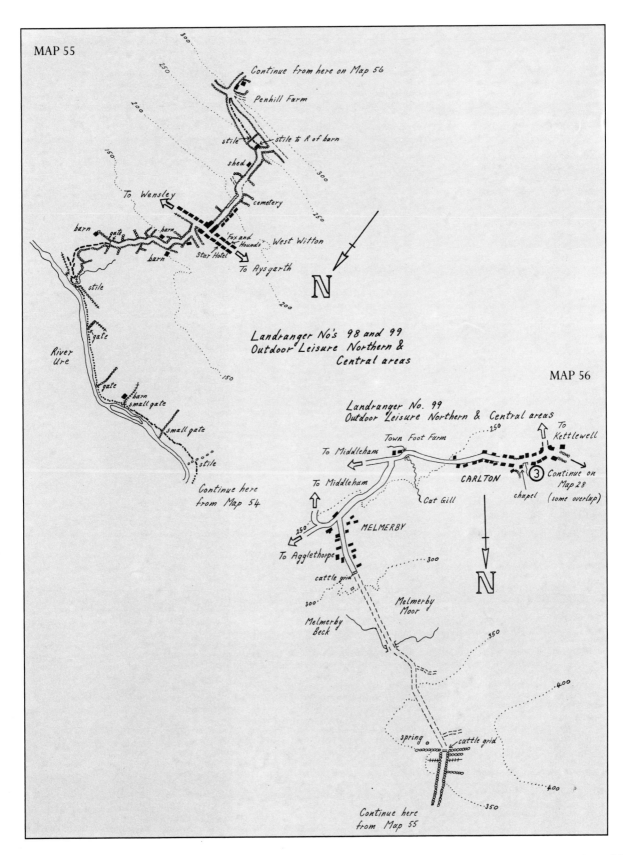

MAP 55

Continue from here on Map 56

Penhill Farm

300
250
200

stile — stile to R of barn

shed

150

To Wensley

cemetery

barn · gate · barn
barn

Fox and Hounds · West Witton

Star Hotel

To Aysgarth

300
250

200

N

River Ure

150

gate

gate

barn
small gate

small gate

stile

Continue here from Map 54

Landranger No's 98 and 99
Outdoor Leisure Northern &
Central areas

MAP 56

Landranger No. 99
Outdoor Leisure Northern & Central areas

Town Foot Farm

250

To Kettlewell

To Middleham

CARLTON

③ Continue on Map 28 (some overlap)

To Middleham

Cat Gill

chapel

MELMERBY

To Agglethorpe

cattle grid

250

Melmerby Moor

300

300

Melmerby Beck

350

N

400

spring · cattle grid

350

400

Continue here from Map 55

165

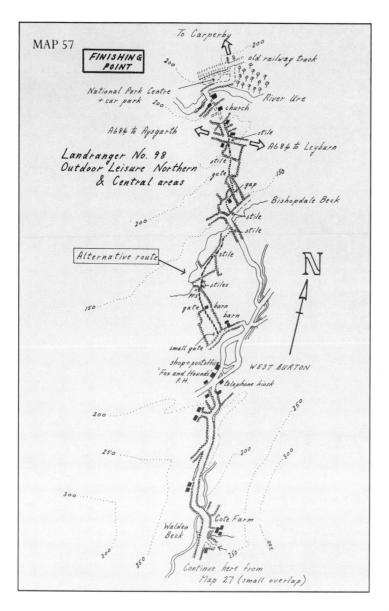

MAP 57

FINISHING POINT

To Carperby
old railway track
National Park Centre + car park
River Ure
church
A684 to Aysgarth
stile
A684 to Leyburn

Landranger No. 98
Outdoor Leisure Northern
& Central areas

stile
gate
gap
Bishopdale Beck
stile
stile

Alternative route

stile

stiles
gate   barn
barn

small gate

shop + post office
'Fox and Hounds' P.H.
telephone kiosk
WEST BURTON

Walden
Beck
Cote Farm

Continue here from
Map 27 (small overlap)

the opposite side to the village of Melmerby. There turn R and shortly, at a T-junction, R again. Go along the road to reach Carlton (3). Continue through the village.

Where the road bends L go to the R up a minor road, and R again up a rough lane after 200 yards (180 m). Follow the lane until it ends, then keep in the same direction with a wall on the L, eventually going through a gap where the wall ends at a corner. Continue on a clear path across the moor, keeping in the same direction, to reach a wall. Follow this wall as it bends L and then R behind an old shooting lodge. 100 yards (75 m) after

Wensleydale from Witton Steeps

166

the lodge, where the wall bends L, continue on a track up the moor to reach a higher wall. Follow this wall and where this also bends L go half R across the moor again to a gap in the wall which runs across the crest of the ridge. On the far side, descend on a path (it broadens) which brings wonderful views over the valley ahead. Eventually reach the end of a wall and swing R. Follow the farm road down into the valley to reach a metalled road by Cote Farm. Turn R along the road to the village of West Burton.

In the village, cross to the road opposite and pass the *Fox and Hounds* public house and the village post office. Continue along the road down to a junction where turn L. At a second junction go R, and finally at a third junction, L along the Aysgarth road (see Map 57 for an alternative route). After $\frac{1}{2}$ mile (800 m) cross a bridge over Bishopdale Beck and turn R. After 25 yards (23 m) turn L through a stile and climb to the L of a barn to a gap in a wall. Continue to a gate in the top corner of the next field. Descend into the valley beyond and then climb up on a path to reach a road to the R of a house. Go down the lane opposite back to the church and car-park.

1 Aysgarth Falls and Carriage Museum   See page 34.

2 The Parish Church of St Andrew, Aysgarth

There has probably been a church at Aysgarth since at least the tenth century, but the present building is the product of a major restoration, carried out in 1856–66, of a church built about 1536. This restoration was so extensive that the base of the tower is the only major part now remaining of the earlier building. Above the south-east door is an old coffin lid of the fourteenth or fifteenth century, possibly that of a verderer of the Forest of Wensleydale, while the Vicar's stall and the screen on the south side were taken from Jervaulx Abbey. There is also a tablet to William Norman Pickles (1885–1969) who was a general practitioner in Wensleydale for over 50 years and an epidemiologist of wide renown.

3 Henry Constantine, the Coverdale Bard   See page 118.

3.27

TAN HILL INN AND
MELBECKS MOOR

STARTING AND FINISHING
POINTS
Keld (92-893012)
LENGTH
18 miles (29 km)
ASCENT
2450 feet (750 m)

A magnificent walk over the great moorland area between Swaledale and Arkengarthdale. Other walkers may be met on the southern stretch where the route coincides with the Coast-to-Coast Walk and to the west where a section of the Pennine Way is followed, but from Hard Level Gill to The Disputes it is likely that few — if any — will be encountered. The path is exceptionally good over most of the route. Old smelt mills at Swinner Gill and Gunnerside Gill, enormous hushes and Tan Hill Inn, the highest in England, are on the way.

ROUTE DESCRIPTION (Maps 16, 58–62 — see also page 92)

Go to the bottom end of the village and turn R along a path just below the church and by a small barn (PFS 'Muker'). After 250 yards (230 m) turn L down a path (by a PW sign) to a footbridge *(1)*. Cross and go up L to meet a farm road. Turn R along it soon crossing a bridge. Follow the farm road for ½ mile (800 m) to where it bends L then R with a wall and a barn to the R. 140 yards (130 m) after the barn fork L at a junction.

Go to the L of a ruined building (Crackpot Hall) and up between a barn and sheep folds to a gate. Continue beyond the gate on a grassy path across the hillside with a ravine down to the R; at the end, descend to a footbridge by a ruin *(2)* at a stream junction. Follow the path which goes up the L-bank of the R-hand stream (East Grain). Near some shooting butts meet a moor road and turn R along it. Follow this for 600 yards (550 m) until it meets a wider moor road coming in from the L, there continue in the same direction. Where it swings R at the top of a huge ravine (this is actually a hush — see The Face of the Yorkshire Dales: Lead Mining page 19) leave the moor road half L and pick up a path which soon becomes clearer. The path crosses the moor to the L of the hush and descends across the hillside into the valley; it reaches the valley floor through zig-zags to the ruins of a smelt mill *(3)* at a stream junction.

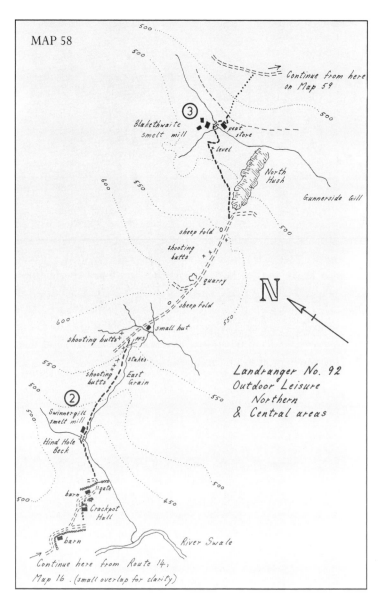

MAP 58

500
500
Continue from here on Map 59
③
Blakethwaite smelt mill
peat store
level
North Hush
Gunnerside Gill
500
550
600
500
sheep fold
shooting butts
quarry
sheep fold
N
small hut
shooting butts
stakes
shooting butts
East Grain
②
Swinnergill smelt mill
Hind Hole Beck

Landranger No. 92
Outdoor Leisure
Northern
& Central areas

550
500
500
550
500

barn
gate
Crackpot Hall
barn
River Swale
450
500

Continue here from Route 14,
Map 16 . (small overlap for clarity)

Cross the footbridge and climb up the hillside ahead to a cross track. Continue to climb (no path) to reach an old mine road. Turn R and follow the mine road across the moor by spoil heaps. After a shooting butt and a ruin on the R, the path crosses a shallow valley then starts to descend towards Hard Level Gill. Where a rough moor road comes in on the R (i.e. by sheep folds and a ruin on the R) turn L on a bearing 344° magnetic, soon crossing a stream and then rising up the moor (no path) to a fence corner.

Continue in the same direction with a fence to your R. After

Upper Swaledale from Crackpot Hall

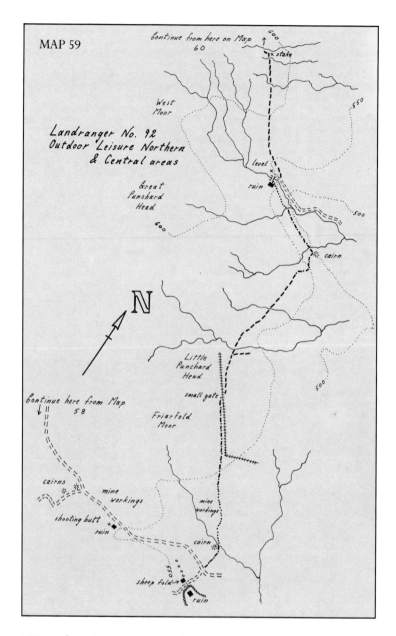

Continue from here on Map 60

MAP 59

West Moor

Landranger No. 92
Outdoor Leisure Northern
& Central areas

Great
Punchard
Head

Continue here from Map 58

Little
Punchard
Head

small gate

Friarfold
Moor

cairns

mine workings

shooting butt

ruin

mine workings

cairn

sheep fold

ruin

500 yards (460 m) cross the fence at a small gate and follow the path away from the fence over the moor. After ½ mile (800 m) the path turns L at a cairn. From this point aim for the small ruin higher up the stream (you will find it easier if you keep to the higher ground on the L). Cross the stream over a small bridge by the ruin and a level and turn R for 50 yards (45 m), then turn back half L up a path. Follow this clear path (cairns) across the moor and then along the moor edge enjoying magnificent views to the R.

Finally, overlooking William Gill continue in the same direction to reach the stream. Cross, turn R, and follow the

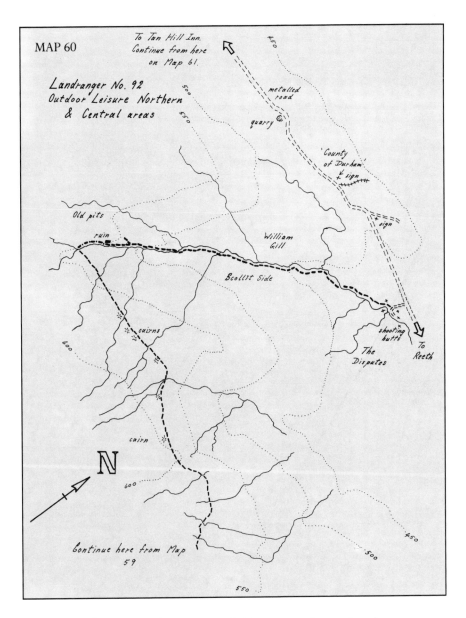

MAP 60

To Tan Hill Inn.
Continue from here
on Map 61.

Landranger No. 92
Outdoor Leisure Northern
& Central areas

metalled
road

quarry

'County
of Durham'
sign

Old pits

ruin

William
Gill

sign

Scollit Side

600

cairns

shooting
butts

The
Disputes

To
Reeth

cairn

N

600

Continue here from Map
59

550

500

450

500

stream for 1½ miles (2.4 km) to a road. Turn L on the road and
walk for 2½ miles (3 km) to Tan Hill Inn *(4)*.

Take the path directly opposite the Inn (PW sign). Follow the
clear path across the moor going R at two path junctions after
about 650 yards (600 m). After about 2 miles (3.2 km) reach a
gate by a barn. Go along the farm road beyond, where this
bends L go ahead to a small gate and continue again across the
open moor on a path. After ½ mile (800 m) pass through a gate
in a fence and later another gate in a wall. Go along the farm
road beyond to a walled lane and down to a farm. Go through a
gate between a house and a barn and continue down the farm
road. Before it goes over a bridge, turn R down a path to a

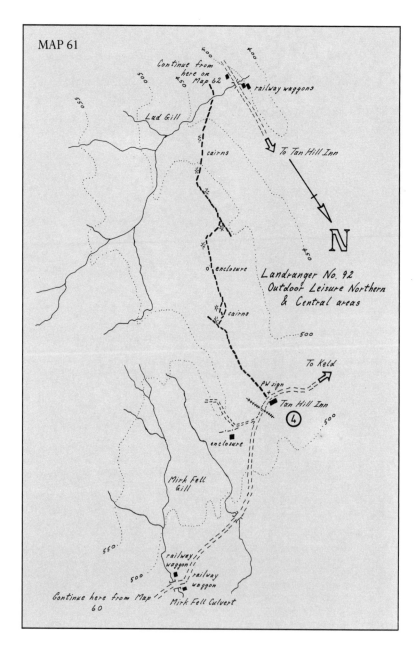

footbridge. Cross and follow the path up the hillside half R to an upper lane, there turn R for Keld.

1 Kisdon Force See page 96.

2 Swinner Gill Smelt Mill

The ruins at the stream junction up Swinner Gill are of a small smelt mill which worked from 1769 to about 1820. The mill was a small rectangular building of two rooms; the right-hand room (facing the mill from East Grain) contained the hearths for smelting and the left-hand room bellows which

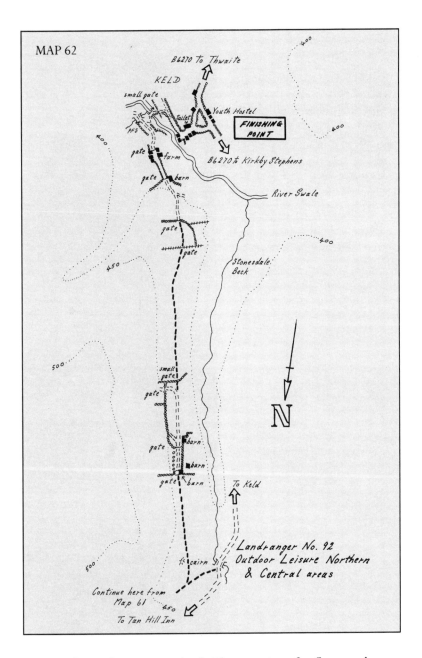

MAP 62

B6270 To Thwaite

KELD

small gate

Youth Hostel

FINISHING
POINT

PFS

gate

farm

B6270 to Kirkby Stephens

gate

barn

River Swale

gate

Stonesdale
Beck

400

gate

450

500

small
gate

gate

gate

barn

barn

gate

barn

To Keld

Landranger No. 92
Outdoor Leisure Northern
& Central areas

cairn

500

Continue here from
Map 61

450

To Tan Hill Inn

were driven by a waterwheel. The remains of a flue can be seen running up the hillside behind the mills.

3 Blakethwaite Mill

The area around Gunnerside Gill is particularly rich in remains from the heyday of the lead mining industry. The head of an enormous hush is reached as you come over the moor top from Swinner Gill and several others are only too obvious on the facing slopes across the valley. The open mouths of levels are passed as you descend and further ruins and spoil heaps can be seen to the right lower in the gill.

The most impressive remains on this route, however, are those of Blakethwaite Mill which are situated at the point where Gunnerside Gill is crossed. The remains of the mill are on the hillside between the two streams with a long flue, cut into solid rock, rising behind. The building by the footbridge, with arches on the stream side, was used as a peat store — the arches giving the air circulation necessary to dry the peat. The mill worked local ores and was in use for about sixty years from 1820.

4 *Tan Hill Inn*

1732 feet (528 km) above sea-level, this is reputed to be the highest inn in England; an important stopping-place for Pennine Way walkers who, approaching over Stonesdale Moor, see it beckoning before them like an oasis with the promise of much-needed refreshment. They are part of a long tradition, for Tan Hill Inn, by the metalled road out of Arkengarthdale and at the crossing point of earlier pack-horse trails, has been serving the needs of travellers for many centuries.

Thin coal seams, low in the Millstone Grit beds, which top the nearby fells, were worked at collieries around Tan Hill from the thirteenth century until last century. (Similar mining also took place on Fountains Fell further to the south.) The coal produced was sent to local towns and in the eighteenth and nineteenth centuries to nearby smelt mills.

A sheep fair is still held by the inn in the third week of May each year.

Tan Hill Inn

THE THREE PEAKS WALK

STARTING AND FINISHING POINT
Horton in Ribblesdale car-park
(98-808724)
LENGTH
23 miles (37 km)
ASCENT
5750 feet (1750m)

The objective of the Three Peaks Walk is to reach the summit cairns of Pen-y-ghent, Whernside and Ingleborough and return to the starting point in a single expedition. Any starting point and route may be chosen, but the vast majority of walkers begin at Horton in Ribblesdale and reach the summits in the order given above. It is generally considered that the feat was first completed in July, 1887 by J. R. Wynne-Edwards and D. R. Smith, in a time of ten hours. Unfortunately, but inevitably, with the passage of many thousands of participants, the route of the Three Peaks Walk has deteriorated to an alarming degree in recent years. This is particularly true of the moorland sections, where the footpaths have been transformed into broad bands of mud. In order to combat this a great deal of resurfacing work has been done recently. Although walking standards have improved in recent years, it is likely that a majority of walkers will still find the Three Peaks Walk to be a considerable undertaking.

A Three Peaks of Yorkshire Club has been formed by Peter and Joyce Bayes for those who have completed the walk within twelve hours. To be eligible for membership walkers must book-out and book-in again at the Pen-y-ghent café, Horton in Ribblesdale, Settle, North Yorkshire; telephone Horton in Ribblesdale (072 96) 333. Complete details should be obtained from the café *before* the attempt.

ROUTE DESCRIPTION
(Maps 12, 63–65, 18–19, 66–69—see also pages 80, 98–99)
Section 1. Horton in Ribblesdale to Pen-y-ghent
Follow Route 12 as far as the summit of Pen-y-ghent.
Section 2. Pen-y-ghent to Whernside
On the summit of Pen-y-ghent cross the wall at a ladder stile and descend to the edge of the steep section where the path bends to the R. Follow the path along the edge gradually descending to reach a large cairn. Here the path bends L and forks. Take the R-hand path and follow it down the moor to a

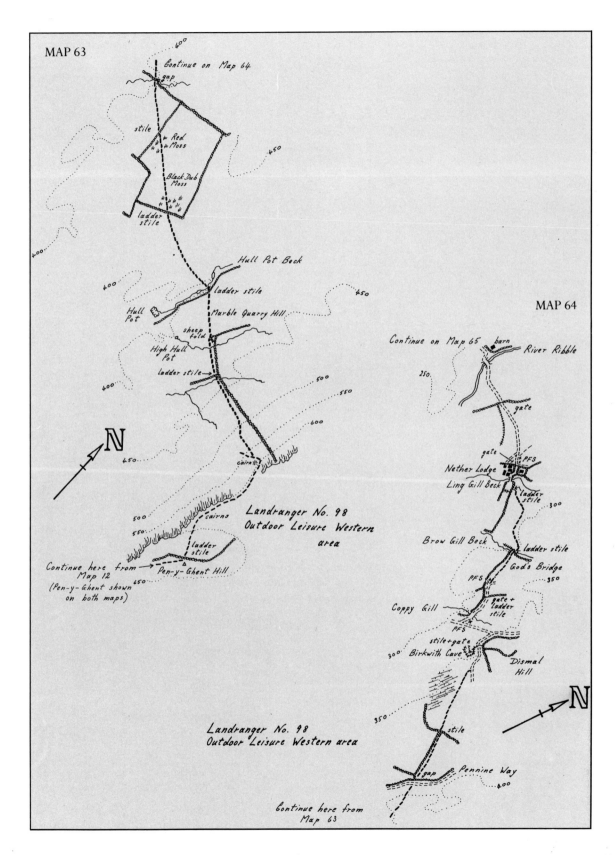

MAP 63

Continue on Map 64

gap

stile

Red Moss

Black Dub Moss

ladder stile

Hull Pot Beck

ladder stile

Marble Quarry Hill

Hull Pot

sheep fold

High Hull Pot

ladder stile

cairns

N

Landranger No. 98
Outdoor Leisure Western area

cairns

ladder stile

Continue here from
Map 12
(Pen-y-Ghent shown
on both maps)

Pen-y-Ghent Hill

Landranger No. 98
Outdoor Leisure Western area

MAP 64

Continue on Map 65   barn   River Ribble

gate

gate   PFS

Nether Lodge

Ling Gill Beck

ladder stile

Brow Gill Beck   ladder stile

God's Bridge

PFS

Coppy Gill   gate + ladder stile

PFS

stile + gate

Birkwith Cave   Dismal Hill

N

stile

gap   Pennine Way

Continue here from
Map 63

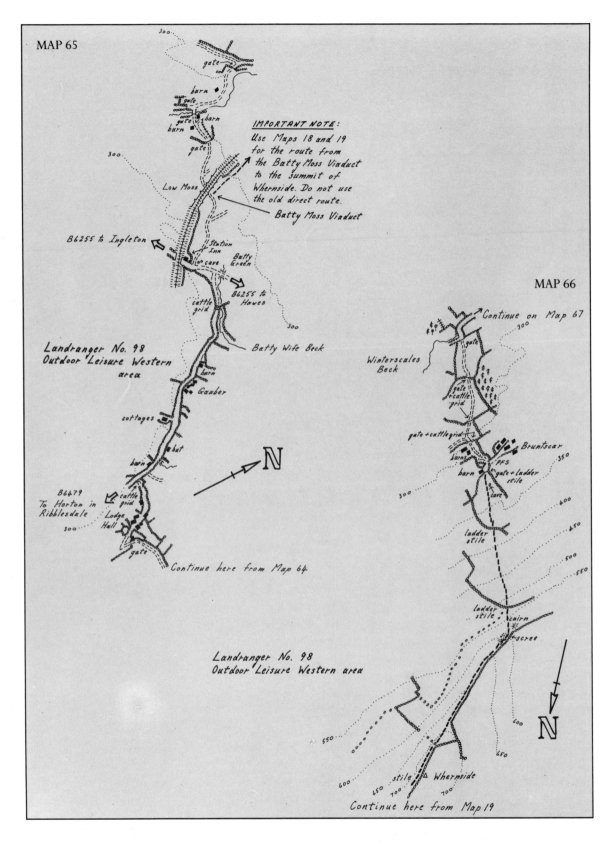

MAP 65

300

gate

barn

gate

gate barn
barn

gate

IMPORTANT NOTE:
Use Maps 18 and 19
for the route from
the Batty Moss Viaduct
to the summit of
Whernside. Do not use
the old direct route.

Low Moss

Batty Moss Viaduct

B6255 to Ingleton

Station
Inn

cave

Batty
Green

B6255 to Hawes

cattle
grid

300

Batty Wife Beck

Landranger No. 98
Outdoor Leisure Western
area

barn

Gauber

cottages

hut

barn

B6479
To Horton in
Ribblesdale

cattle
grid

Lodge
Hall

300

gate

Continue here from Map 64

N

MAP 66

Continue on Map 67

300

Winterscales
Beck

gate

gate
+cattle
grid

gate+cattle grid

barn

Bruntscar

PFS
gate + ladder
stile

350

barn

cave

300

400

ladder
stile

450

500

550

ladder
stile   cairn

scree

600

Landranger No. 98
Outdoor Leisure Western area

N

550

600

650

600

650 700

stile △ Whernside

700

Continue here from Map 19

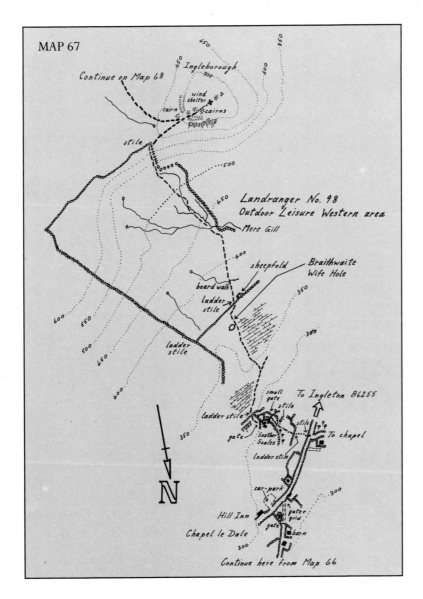

MAP 67

Continue on Map 68

Ingleborough

wind
shelter

cairn   cairns

stile

Landranger No. 98
Outdoor Leisure Western area

Mere Gill

sheepfold   Braithwaite
                 Wife Hole
board walk

ladder
stile

ladder
stile

N

small
gate   To Ingleton B6255
      stile
ladder stile
              stile
gate   To chapel
      Souther
      Scales

ladder stile

car-park

Hill Inn   cater
                  grid
Chapel le Dale gate   barn

Continue here from Map 66

stream. Cross. (Note: if the stream is in flood then a detour will
have to be made downstream to Hull Pot, where the stream
sinks, returning on the opposite bank.) Continue in the same
direction on a clear path up the moor, to reach a crossing wall at
a ladder stile. Keep going, still in the same direction, over the
next stretch of moor to a stile in a wall. (Care is necessary here
as particularly unpleasant bogs — Black Dub Moss and Red
Moss — lie across the path at both ends of this stretch of moor;
in each case it is best to make a considerable detour around the
boggy areas, rejoining the path further along). Continue along
the path across the moor to a wall gap and then later descend to
a further gap. (The green lane crossing here is part of the
Pennine Way going from Horton in Ribblesdale to Hawes.)

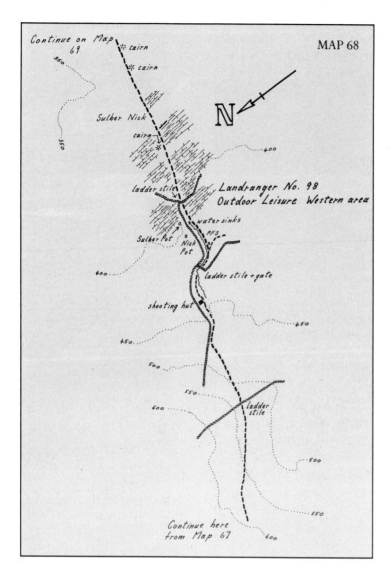

MAP 68

Continue on Map 69

Sulber Nick

Landranger No. 98
Outdoor Leisure Western area

ladder stile

water sinks

Sulber Pot
Nick Pot

ladder stile + gate

shooting hut

ladder stile

Continue here from Map 67

From the gap, climb to the R of a wall to a stile. Continue on the green path beyond by limestone pavements to join a farm road, follow this to a T-junction where you go L. At the next junction (PFS 'Nether Lodge') turn R and follow a farm road by a wall. Where the farm road swings R, continue with the wall to a ladder stile at a natural bridge over a stream (appropriately named 'God's Bridge'). Follow the footpath beyond towards a farm (Nether Lodge). Cross a ladder stile and then a bridge and go between the house and barns. At a gate by the house reach a farm road. Follow this farm road for 1 mile (1.6 km) crossing the infant Ribble and passing Lodge Hall to reach a main road

Chapel-le-Dale from Ingleborough

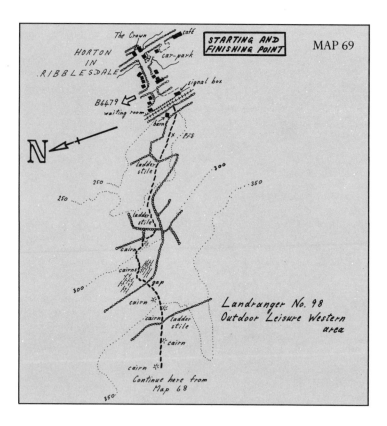

(B6479). Turn R to the T-junction at Ribblehead. Now use Route 15 from Ribblehead to the summit of Whernside.

Section 3. Whernside to Ingleborough

Continue along the summit ridge, going in the same direction. About ¾ mile (1.2 km) from the summit descend over two small patches of scree; at the bottom of the second patch by a large cairn go half L and descend the steep face to a ladder stile. Continue descending to a second ladder stile and then over a field to a third ladder stile in the far R-hand corner. Enter a lane and follow it to the R for a few yards, then L through a gate on to a metalled road. Follow this to the main road (B6255) at Chapel-le-Dale. Turn R down the road.

Opposite the entrance road to Chapel-le-Dale church, go L over a stile (PFS 'Ingleborough'). (This is a very long route and most walkers will by now have both the time and the distance still to be covered to the end at Horton in Ribblesdale very much in mind. Chapel-le-Dale church, however, is a small but charming building which has an interesting connection with the Settle–Carlisle Railway passed earlier in the day. It is but a very short detour away to the right.) Cross the field to a ladder stile and then up through trees and a scar to a stile in a fence. Continue to a small gate to the R of a house and then bend half L through a gap (i.e. to the R of a barn). Go through a gate ahead then R uphill crossing a limestone scar and a ladder stile. Turn R above the scar and after about 300 yards (280 m) turn L up a second scar. At the top follow a path curving R to pass a large sink hole (Braithwaite Wife Hole) to the R. Shortly afterwards, cross at a double ladder stile by a sheepfold and just beyond a board walk. Keep in the same direction along a path which later bends half L. Climb steadily up the moor, later more steeply, to reach the top of the ridge. Turn R, cross a stile and climb up the final summit rise ahead. On the top, cross to the summit cairn.

Section 4. Ingleborough to Horton in Ribblesdale

Return by the same route. Just below the edge fork R on an obvious path. Follow this path across the moor to a ladder stile in a wall. Later, meet a further wall and continue with it on your L soon passing a shooting hut and crossing a wall on the way. Where the wall ends (soon after water sinks) continue ahead along Sulber Nick crossing a pavement area (cairns). After 1 mile (1.6 km) reach a ladder stile, and then after 350 yards (320 m) go through a gap in a wall. The faint path beyond bends half R and then descends L (cairns) to a ladder stile in a wall corner. Cross the field beyond to a second ladder stile. Cross a further two fields to reach a railway track. Cross (with care!) and go down the station road to the main road (B6479). Continue ahead to the car-park in Horton in Ribblesdale where you started much earlier in the day.

APPENDICES

Access for the Walker

It is important to realize that the designation of a National Park does not change the ownership of the land within it in any way. In the case of the Yorkshire Dales National Park, for example, less than one per cent of the land is under any form of public ownership. The laws of access and trespass apply just as much to areas of private land within a National Park as to those outside it.

The National Parks and Access to the Country-side Act of 1949 required County Councils in England and Wales to prepare maps which showed all paths over which the public had a right to walk. The final form of the map is referred to as a definitive map and copies are held at the offices of the County Council and District Council and sometimes by the Parish Council concerned. Public Paths can only be diverted or deleted from a definitive map by the raising of a Diversion Order or an Extinguishment Order respectively. The paths are classified as either footpaths (for walkers only) or bridleways (for walkers, horser-iders and cyclists). These public paths were included on the now withdrawn one inch to one mile (1:63 360) Seventh Series, most 1:25 000 Second Series (i.e. Pathfinder), 1:50 000 First and Second Series (i.e. Landranger) and the Outdoor Leisure maps.

A 'road used as a public path' is a highway, other than a public path, used by the public mainly for the purpose for which footpaths or bridleways are used. They may still be shown as such on Ordnance Survey maps, although they are being reclassified on definitive maps as either footpaths, bridleways or byways open to all traffic. In any event a public right-of-way exists. Further-more, many unmetalled roads (fenced and unfenced) which give excellent walking are open to the public, although the Ordnance Survey map does not specifically show them as having public rights-of-way.

Although there are a large number of footpaths and bridleways within the area of the Park, there are also substantial areas where none exists. Fortunately, however, access may also be permit-ted to such areas under one of the following:

ACCESS AGREEMENTS
Under the National Park and Access to the Countryside Act of 1949, National Park Authori-ties have the power to negotiate Access Agree-ments with landowners whereby access is given in return for compensation in the form of a grant. This access may be subject to conditions as appropriate to the area.

An agreement has been made between the Trustees of the Chatsworth Settlement and the North Yorkshire County Council giving access to about 14,000 acres (5700 hectares) of Barden Moor and Barden Fell around the Wharfe Valley. Walkers are asked to leave these areas at certain Access Points where copies of the bye-laws are on display, camping is not permitted nor are dogs allowed. The areas may also be closed by the owners on not more than 30 days each year, the dates being publicized at Access Points; in practice these occur between August and December.

NATIONAL TRUST PROPERTIES
The Trust policy is to give free access at all times to its open spaces; however there cannot be unrestricted access to tenanted farms, young plantations and woods, or certain nature reserves where the preservation of rare fauna and flora is paramount.

The public has access to the south-east shore of Malham Tarn which is owned by the Trust.

PERMISSIVE PATHS

A number of footpaths on land in the Bolton Abbey area, held by the Trustees of the Chatsworth Settlement, have been opened for public use, although not in themselves having legal rights-of-way. These are all signposted and waymarked. Information can be obtained from the information kiosk at Cavendish Pavilion near Bolton Abbey.

Access is allowed, on payment of a small fee, to the lakeside path from Clapham to Ingleborough Cave (Routes 5 and 13), to those of the Waterfalls Walk (Route 6) and to Hardraw Force (Route 7).

YORKSHIRE WATER AUTHORITY

Walkers are allowed to cross the dam of Upper Barden Reservoir — but not Lower Barden — on the Barden Moors; also to part of the shore line of Grimwith Reservoir.

TRADITION

Walkers have for very many years walked freely in some of the hill and mountain areas of the Park with the tacit agreement of the landowners concerned, even though they may have had no legal right to do so. The tolerance shown will vary from farmer to farmer and, in any case, depends for its continuation upon the sensible behaviour of the walkers themselves. Litter, broken glass, ruined walls, unruly dogs, noisy behaviour, etc. are likely to make it more difficult for the next people to go that way.

It must be pointed out however that in some areas of the Dales landowners have firmly resisted access upon their land. Finally, most forestry plantations within the Park are privately owned; there is no access in these areas except by public right-of-way.

An excellent guide for the general public, *Out in the country. Where you can go and what you can do,* has been published by the Countryside Commission (see page 190).

Safety

The golden rules for safety in mountain and moorland areas are:

DO

Carry appropriate clothing and equipment, which should be in a sound condition.

Carry map and compass and be practised in their use.

Leave a note of your intended route with a responsible person (and keep to it!).

Report your return as soon as possible.

Keep warm, but not overwarm, at all times.

Eat nourishing foods and rest at regular intervals.

Avoid becoming exhausted.

Know First Aid and the correct procedure in case of accidents or illness.

Obtain a weather forecast before you start.

DO NOT

Go out on your own unless you are very experienced; three is a good number.

Leave any member of the party behind on a mountain or moor unless help has to be summoned.

Explore old mine workings or caves or climb cliffs (except scrambling ridges).

Attempt routes which are beyond your skill and experience.

Giving a Grid Reference

Giving a grid reference is an excellent way of 'pin-pointing' a feature, such as a church or mountain summit, on an Ordnance Survey map.

Grid lines, which are used for this purpose, are shown on the 1:25 000 Outdoor Leisure, 1:25 000 Pathfinder and 1:50 000 Landranger maps produced by the Ordnance Survey; these are the maps most commonly used by walkers. Grid lines are the thin blue lines one kilometre apart going vertically and horizontally across the map producing a network of small squares. Each line, whether vertical or horizontal, is given a number from 00 to 99, with the sequence repeating itself every 100 lines. The 00 lines are slightly thicker than the others thus producing large squares each side representing 100 km and made up of 100 small squares. Each of these large squares is identified by two letters. The entire network of lines covering the British Isles, excluding Ireland, is called the National Grid.

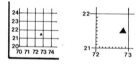

FIGURE 5 Giving a grid reference

The left-hand diagram of Figure 5 shows a corner of an Ordnance Survey 1:50 000 Landranger map which contains a Youth Hostel. Using this map, the method of determining a grid reference is as follows:

Step 1.
Holding the map in the normal upright position, note the number of the 'vertical' grid line to the left of the hostel. This is 72.
Step 2.
Now imagine that the space between this grid line and the adjacent one to the right of the hostel is divided into ten equal divisions (the diagram on the right does this for you). Estimate the number of these 'tenths' that the hostel lies to the right of the left-hand grid line. This is 8. Add this to the number found in Step 1 to make 728.
Step 3.
Note the number of the grid line below the hostel and add it on to the number obtained above. This is 21, so that the number becomes 72821.
Step 4.
Repeat Step 2 for the space containing the hostel, but now in a vertical direction. The final number to be added is 5, making 728215. This is called a six-figure grid reference. This, coupled with the number or name of the appropriate Landranger or Outdoor Leisure map, will enable the Youth Hostel to be found.

A full grid reference will also include the identification of the appropriate 100 kilometre square of the National Grid; for example, SD 728215. This information is given in the margin of each map.

Countryside Access Charter

YOUR RIGHTS OF WAY ARE
Public footpaths — on foot only. Sometimes way-marked in yellow
Bridleways — on foot, horseback and pedal cycle. Sometimes waymarked in blue
Byways (usually old roads), most 'Roads Used as Public Paths' and, of course, public roads — all traffic
Use maps, signs and waymarks. Ordnance Survey Pathfinder and Landranger maps show most public rights of way.

ON RIGHTS OF WAY YOU CAN
Take a pram, pushchair or wheelchair if practicable
Take a dog (on a lead or under close control)
Take a short route round an illegal obstruction or remove it sufficiently to get past

YOU HAVE A RIGHT TO GO FOR RECREATION TO
Public parks and open spaces — on foot
Most commons near older towns and cities — on foot and sometimes on horseback
Private land where the owner has a formal agreement with the local authority

IN ADDITION YOU CAN USE BY ESTABLISHED CUSTOM OR CONSENT BUT ASK FOR ADVICE IF YOU ARE UNSURE

Many areas of open country like moorland, fell and coastal areas, especially those of the National Trust, and some commons
Some woods and forests, especially those owned by the Forestry Commission
Country Parks and picnic sites
Most beaches
Canal towpaths

Some private paths and tracks. Consent sometimes extends to riding horses and pedal cycles

FOR YOUR INFORMATION:
County councils and London boroughs maintain and record rights of way, and register commons
Obstructions, dangerous animals, harassment and misleading signs on rights of way are illegal and you should report them to the county council
Paths across fields can be ploughed, but must normally be reinstated within two weeks
Landowners can require you to leave land to which you have no right of access
Motor vehicles are normally permitted only on roads, byways and some 'Roads Used as Public Paths'
Follow any local bylaws

AND, WHEREVER YOU GO, FOLLOW THE COUNTRY CODE:
Enjoy the countryside and respect its life and work
Guard against all risk of fire
Fasten all gates
Keep your dogs under close control
Keep to public paths across farmland
Use gates and stiles to cross fences, hedges and walls
Leave livestock, crops and machinery alone
Take your litter home
Help to keep all water clean
Protect wildlife, plants and trees
Take special care on country roads
Make no unnecessary noise.

This Charter is for practical guidance in England and Wales only. It was prepared by the Countryside Commission.

Addresses of Useful Organizations

The Camping and Caravanning Club,
11 Lower Grosvenor Place,
London,
SW1W 0EY.
01-828 1012.

Countryside Commission,
John Dower House,
Crescent Place,
Cheltenham,
Gloucestershire, GL50 3RA.
Cheltenham (0242) 521381.

Council for National Parks,
45 Shelton Street,
London, WC2H 9HJ.
01-240 3603.

The Dalesman Publishing Co. Ltd.,
Clapham,
via Lancaster,
North Yorkshire.
For books on the life of the Dales.

The Long Distance Walkers Association.
Kevin Uzzell – Membership Secretary,
7 Ford Drive,
Yarnfield,
Stone,
Staffordshire ST15 0RP.
Stafford (0785) 7606 84.

The National Trust,
36 Queen Anne's Gate,
London, SW1H 9AS.
01-222 9251.
(Regional Information Officer,
Miss T. Hunt,
The Yorkshire Regional Office of the National
Trust,
The Goddards,
27 Tadcaster Road,
Dringhouses,
York, YO2 2QG.
York (0904) 702021.)

Rambler's Association,
1/5 Wandsworth Road,
London, SW8 2XX.
01-582 6878.

The Yorkshire and Humberside Tourist Board,
312 Tadcaster Road,
York,
North Yorkshire, YO2 2HF.
York (0904) 707961.

Yorkshire Dales National Park,
'Colvend',
Hebden Road,
Grassington,
Skipton,
North Yorkshire, BD23 5LB.
Grassington (0756) 752748.
For all orders by post of National Park
publications and for all telephone and postal
enquiries.

Yorkshire Dales Society,
152 Main Street,
Addingham,
Ilkley,
West Yorkshire, LS29 0LY.
Ilkley (0943) 607868.

Youth Hostels Association (England and Wales),
Trevelyan House,
8 St Stephen's Hill,
St Albans,
Hertfordshire, AL1 2DY.
St Albans (0727) 55215.

INDEX

Place names and sites of interest only are included. Page numbers in *italics* refer to illustrations.

Appletreewick 17
Arant Haw 139, *143*
Arkengarthdale 133–8, 169
Arncliffe 75, 77, 145, *149*, 151–6
Aysgarth Falls 10, 33–6, 163, 168

Barden
    Bridge 132
    Fell 127
    Moor 157–62
    Reservoir 162
    Tower 160, 162
Batty Moss Viaduct *see* Ribblehead Viaduct
Beezley Falls 52
Blakethwaite Mill 18, 120, 175
Bolton Abbey 70–4, 127
    Priory 72, *73*
    Woods *74*
Bolton Castle 33, 34, 36
Brackenbottom 79
Buckden 59, *61*, 63, 145

Calf, The 139–144
Calver Hill 133
Carlton 163
    Moor 115–18, 119, 163
Castley 139
Cautley
    Holme Beck 37
    Spout 37–40, *41*
Cavendish Memorial Fountain 72
Caves *see* Northern Pennine Cave Area
Chapel-le-Dale *183*, 184
Churn Milk Hole 79
Clapham 10, *47*, 48, 84, 103
    Beck 45–8
Corpse Way 96
Coverdale 115, 163–8
Cray 17, 59
Crina Bottom 84, *87*
Cross Keys Temperance Hotel 37, *39*
Crummack Dale 103–7

Disputes, The 169
Doe 49

Fleensop Moor 115
Force Gill 97
Fremington Edge 133

Gaping Gill 19, 46, 84, 85–6, 88
Gordale Scar 30, 31, 64–8, 108
Grassington 10
Green Dragon, The 54, 55
Greenhow Hill 17
Gunnerside 94, 120–6
    Gill 124–6, 169

Hard Level Gills 120, 169
Hardraw Force 54–8
Hawes 10, 36, 54
Hawkswick Moor 75–8
Horton in Ribblesdale 79, 178, 185
Howgills 37, 127, 139–144
Hubberholme 59, *62*, 63
Hull Pot 80, 82
Hunt Pot 80, 82

Ingleborough 84–9, 178–85
    Cave 45–8
    geology 15, 17
    Hall 46, 48
Ingleton 84
    geology 15
    Glens Walk 49–53

Janet's Foss 66–7

Keld 17, 90, 91, 94
Kettlewell 75
Kilnsey 151, 156
Kisdon Force 96

Langthwaite 133
Leyburn-Hawes Railway 36
Little Gordale 66–7
Littondale 75, 145

Malham 10, 12, 20, *113*
    Cove 28–32, *29*, *31*, 64–8
    geology 15, 17
    Moor 108–114, 151
    Tarn 30, 108, 112
    Tarn House 112–13
Marrick 17
Marsett 44
Mastiles Lane 151–6
Melbecks Moor 120, 169–76
Melmerby 163
Moor End Fell 145
Muker 90, 91, 94
    Church 96

Nappa Scars 107
Norber Erratics 103–7
Northern Pennine Cave Area 19

Old Cote Moor 145
Old Gang Mine 18, 120, *123*, 126

Pecca Falls 49–50
Pen-y-ghent 79–82, *83*, 178–85
    geology 15
Pennine Way 113–14, 171

Reeth 133, *135*
Ribblehead 97
    Viaduct 100
Rylstone 157, 158, *161*

Sedbergh 10, 37, 139
Semer Water 42–4
Settle 15
    -Carlisle Railway 99
Shaw Gill Wood 58
Simon's Seat 127–32
Skirwith Quarry 53
Starbotton 145
Strid, The 70–4, 128
Stump Cross Caverns 46
Surrender 18
    Bridge 120
    Smelt Mill 121, 126
Swaledale 17, 169
    geology 15
    Upper 90–6, 171
Swinner Gill 169, 174–5

Tan Hill Inn 169–77
Thornton Force 49, 50, *51*, 52
Thorpe Fell Top 157
Three Peaks Walk 178–85
Thwaite 90, *93*, 94, 95–6
Trow Gill 84
Twiss 49, *53*

Upper Dales Folk Museum 56
Upper Wharfedale *see* Wharfedale

Valley of Desolation 127, *129*, 130

Walden Beck 115, 116
Water Sinks 109, 114
Watlowes *111*
Watt Crag 158
Wensleydale 163–8
    geology 15
    Railway 56
West Burton 163
Wharfedale 17, 75, 145
    Upper 59–63
Whernside 97–102, 178–85
White Fell 139
White Scar Cave 46

Yore Mill 34
Yorkshire Dales National Park 9–11
    Centres 10